"This series is a tremendous resource for [understanding of how the gospel is wove] pastors and scholars doing gospel business from all the Scriptures. This is a biblical and theological feast preparing God's people to apply the entire Bible to all of life with heart and mind wholly committed to Christ's priorities."

BRYAN CHAPELL, pastor; author, *Christ-Centered Preaching* and *Christ-Centered Worship*

"Mark Twain may have smiled when he wrote to a friend, 'I didn't have time to write you a short letter, so I wrote you a long letter.' But the truth of Twain's remark remains serious and universal, because well-reasoned, compact writing requires extra time and extra hard work. And this is what we have in the Crossway Bible study series *Knowing the Bible*. The skilled authors and notable editors provide the contours of each book of the Bible as well as the grand theological themes that bind them together as one Book. Here, in a 12-week format, are carefully wrought studies that will ignite the mind and the heart."

R. KENT HUGHES, Senior Pastor Emeritus, College Church, Wheaton, Illinois

"*Knowing the Bible* brings together a gifted team of Bible teachers to produce a high-quality series of study guides. The coordinated focus of these materials is unique: biblical content, provocative questions, systematic theology, practical application, and the gospel story of God's grace presented all the way through Scripture."

PHILIP G. RYKEN, President, Wheaton College

"These *Knowing the Bible* volumes provide a significant and very welcome variation on the general run of inductive Bible studies. This series provides substantial instruction, as well as teaching through the very questions that are asked. *Knowing the Bible* then goes even further by showing how any given text links with the gospel, the whole Bible, and the formation of theology. I heartily endorse this orientation of individual books to the whole Bible and the gospel, and I applaud the demonstration that sound theology was not something invented later by Christians, but is right there in the pages of Scripture."

GRAEME L. GOLDSWORTHY, former lecturer in Old Testament, Biblical Theology, and Hermeneutics, Moore Theological College

"What a gift to earnest, Bible-loving, Bible-searching believers! The organization and structure of the Bible study format presented through the *Knowing the Bible* series is so well conceived. Students of the Word are led to understand the content of passages through perceptive, guided questions, and they are given rich insights and application all along the way in the brief but illuminating sections that conclude each study. What potential growth in depth and breadth of understanding these studies offer! One can only pray that vast numbers of believers will discover more of God and the beauty of his Word through these rich studies."

BRUCE A. WARE, T. Rupert and Lucille Coleman Professor of Christian Theology, The Southern Baptist Theological Seminary

KNOWING THE BIBLE

Douglas Sean O'Donnell, Series Editor

•   •   •   •   •   •

Genesis

Exodus

Leviticus

Numbers

Deuteronomy

Joshua

Judges

Ruth and Esther

1–2 Samuel

1–2 Kings

1–2 Chronicles

Ezra and Nehemiah

Job

Psalms

Proverbs

Ecclesiastes

Song of Solomon

Isaiah

Jeremiah

Lamentations, Habakkuk,
and Zephaniah

Ezekiel

Daniel

Hosea

Joel, Amos, and Obadiah

Jonah, Micah, and Nahum

Haggai, Zechariah, and
Malachi

Matthew

Mark

Luke

John

Acts

Romans

1 Corinthians

2 Corinthians

Galatians

Ephesians

Philippians

Colossians and Philemon

1–2 Thessalonians

1–2 Timothy and Titus

Hebrews

James

1–2 Peter and Jude

1–3 John

Revelation

The Ten Commandments   The Sermon on the Mount   The Parables of Jesus

•   •   •   •   •   •

DOUGLAS SEAN O'DONNELL (PhD, University of Aberdeen) is the Senior Vice President of Bible Editorial at Crossway. He is the author and editor of more than a dozen books, including *The Beginning and End of Wisdom*; *The Pastor's Book*; *The Song of Solomon* and *Matthew* in the Preaching the Word commentary series; and *Psalms* and *The Parables of Jesus* in the *Knowing the Bible* series. He also contributed "Song of Solomon" and "Job" to the ESV Expository Commentary.

THE SERMON ON THE MOUNT

A 12-WEEK STUDY

Drew Hunter

WHEATON, ILLINOIS

Knowing the Bible: The Sermon on the Mount, A 12-Week Study

Copyright © 2023 by Crossway

Published by Crossway
        1300 Crescent Street
        Wheaton, Illinois 60187

Some content used in this study guide has been adapted from the *ESV Study Bible*, copyright © 2008 by Crossway, pages 1827–1835. Used by permission. All rights reserved.

Cover design: Simplicated Studio

First printing 2023

Printed in the United States of America

Scripture quotations are from the ESV® Bible (The Holy Bible, English Standard Version®), copyright © 2001 by Crossway, a publishing ministry of Good News Publishers. Used by permission. All rights reserved.

All emphases in Scripture quotations have been added by the author.

Trade paperback ISBN: 978-1-4335-8940-9

EPub ISBN: 978-1-4335-8943-0
PDF ISBN: 978-1-4335-8941-6

Crossway is a publishing ministry of Good News Publishers.

VP			33	32	31	30	29	28	27	26	25	24	23
15	14	13	12	11	10	9	8	7	6	5	4	3	2	1

TABLE OF CONTENTS

▲

SERIES PREFACE

KNOWING THE BIBLE, as the title indicates, was created to help readers know and understand the meaning, the message, and the God of the Bible. This series was created and edited by Lane Dennis and Dane Ortlund, and J. I. Packer served as the theological editor. Dr. Packer has gone to be with the Lord, Lane has retired as CEO and president of Crossway, and Dane now serves as senior pastor of Naperville (Illinois) Presbyterian Church. We are so grateful for their labors in overseeing the first forty-plus volumes of this series! To honor and expand upon their idea, we are continuing the series, focusing on key sections from Scripture, such as the Ten Commandments and the Sermon on the Mount.

Each volume in the series consists of twelve units that progressively take the reader through a clear, concise, and deep study of certain portions of Scripture. The material works best for a small group, as the questions are designed for good interactive group discussion. Even so, an individual could easily use the material for a personal Bible study as well.

Week 1 provides an overview of the section or sections of Scripture to be studied, which includes placing the text into its larger context (e.g., the Sermon on the Mount within the Gospel of Matthew), providing key historical background, and offering some questions to get started. Weeks 2–12 each have the following features: a summary of how the text fits into the rest of Scripture ("The Place of the Passage"), a summary sentence on the main theme ("The Big Picture"), and ten or so questions ("Reflection and Discussion Questions"). Moreover, each unit highlights the role of the gospel of grace in each text ("Gospel Glimpses"), identifies whole-Bible themes ("Whole-Bible Connections"), pinpoints Christian doctrines ("Theological Soundings"), defines key terms ("Definitions"), and allows space to respond ("Personal Implications").

Lastly, to help readers understand the Bible better, we urge readers to use the ESV Bible and the ESV *Study Bible*, which are available in various print and digital formats, including online editions at esv.org. The *Knowing the Bible* series is also available online.

May our gracious God, who has generously given his Spirit and his Word, use this study to grow his people in their knowledge and love of the Father, Son, and Spirit.

Douglas Sean O'Donnell
Series Editor

WEEK 1: OVERVIEW

Getting Acquainted

Jesus' teaching in the Sermon on the Mount has left an incredible impact throughout history and across the world. Some of Jesus' most well-known sayings come from this section of teaching, such as the Beatitudes, the Lord's Prayer, the Golden Rule, and sayings such as "turn the other cheek," "judge not, that you be not judged," and "you are the light of the world." Yet Jesus offers much more than nuggets of disconnected instruction here. In this sermon he authoritatively unfolds his vision of true flourishing. Jesus has brought the kingdom of God[1] into the world, and this sermon describes the new kind of community he is creating.

Jesus does not call us to earn our salvation through living in the way he describes, nor are his commands intended merely to lead us to despair of ever obeying them. Instead, Jesus shows how his forgiven and transformed people live as a new humanity. This is the new and beautiful culture of his kingdom. He is the king, this is his vision, and he invites us to enter through grace and to obey in the power of his Spirit. In the end, he calls us to decisiveness: will we humbly receive this wisdom and build our lives upon his teaching, or will we reject his authority, wisdom, and grace?

Placing It in the Larger Story

The Sermon on the Mount plays an important role in an epic story. God created the world to flourish with communal joy (Genesis 1–2). However, Adam and Eve chose folly over wisdom, which led to a world of disordered values (Genesis 3). From there, the Old Testament Scriptures unfold the story of God's grace for sinners and sufferers. This is a drama that holds out the hope of a renewed world: the new creation,[2] the kingdom of God, a world of flourishing and joy. Jesus comes as the one true king, and he announces the beginning of this restoration: "Repent, for the kingdom of heaven is at hand" (Matt. 4:17). He goes on to live a perfectly faithful life, die in the place of sinners, rise as the world's true king, and pour out his Spirit to transform his people, and he will one day return to renew all things. He has given the Sermon on the Mount to summarize the new life that his Spirit will empower his people to live. This is the joyful flourishing he has created us for all along.

Key Verse

"Everyone then who hears these words of mine and does them will be like a wise man who built his house on the rock" (Matt. 7:24).

Date and Historical Background

The Sermon on the Mount is Matthew's summary of a portion of Jesus' teaching. Jesus communicated the original instruction to his disciples on a mountain (Matt. 5:1), and by the end many other people have come to listen (7:28). We do not know how much or for how long Jesus taught on this occasion, but Matthew includes the essentials for the purpose of his Gospel account. Luke includes similar examples of Jesus' teaching (Luke 6:20–49), from which we can infer that Jesus taught many of his lessons on various occasions.

Matthew wrote his account of the gospel in the late AD 50s or early 60s. The Sermon on the Mount preserves the vision for true flourishing that Jesus calls his people to cultivate, even amid persecution.

Outline

The Sermon the Mount is not a disorganized collection of sayings but a series of naturally progressing sections. Some sections have clear introductory or concluding statements. Others function as hinges, looking backward to what has come before and introducing what follows. In the introduction Jesus calls his people to true flourishing and faithful witness in the world (Matt. 5:1–16). In the next section Jesus affirms that he fulfills Scripture, and he calls his people to a greater righteousness than that of the teachers of Israel (5:17–20). Jesus explains this greater righteousness in the realm of six ethical topics (5:21–48) and three areas of devotion (6:1–18). He then applies this vision to various aspects of life in the world (6:19–7:12). He concludes with a series of contrasts that urge hearers to embrace the wisdom of his words (7:13–27).

I. Introduction: The Call to Flourishing and Faithful Witness (5:1–16)

   A. The Beatitudes: An Invitation to True Flourishing (5:1–12)

   B. Living as Salt and Light in the World (5:13–16)

II. Fulfillment of Scripture and Call to a Greater Righteousness (5:17–20)

III. The Greater Righteousness Explained with Six Topics (5:21–48)

   A. Anger (5:21–27)

   B. Lust (5:28–30)

   C. Divorce (5:31–32)

   D. Oaths (5:33–37)

   E. Retaliation (5:38–42)

   F. Love (5:43–48)

IV. The Greater Righteousness Explained with Three Areas of Devotion (6:1–18)

   A. Giving (6:1–4)

   B. Prayer (6:5–15)

   C. Fasting (6:16–18)

V. The Greater Righteousness in Relation to Material Things (6:19–34)

   A. Replacing Greed with Generosity (6:19–24)

   B. Replacing Anxiety with Trust (6:25–34)

VI. The Greater Righteousness in Our Relationships (7:1–12)

   A. Relationships in the Church and the World (7:1–6)

   B. Relationship with God (7:7–11)

   C. The Golden Rule (7:12)

VII. Conclusion: A Call to Wisdom and Decisiveness (7:13–27)

   A. Two Ways (7:13–14)

   B. Two Trees (7:15–20)

    C. Two Claims (7:21–23)

    D. Two Foundations (7:24–27)

VIII. Astonishment at Jesus' Authority (7:28–29)

As You Get Started

Have you engaged with the Sermon on the Mount before, either from reading, conversation, or teaching? If so, what are a few things that come to mind that you already know about this sermon? If not, on what do you expect Jesus to focus?

Take a few minutes to skim through the contents of the Sermon on the Mount (or consider reading through it, which takes only 15 to 20 minutes). What words does Jesus repeat? What themes does he emphasize? How would you summarize the overall tone of the whole sermon?

What parts of Jesus' teaching do you expect to be the most personally challenging for you? What do you expect to be the most countercultural in light of the society in which you live?

What are a couple of specific questions that you hope this study will answer concerning Jesus, his ethical teaching, or what it means to live as a Christian?

What is one statement that stood out to you from scanning the Sermon on the Mount that you are eager to explore or put into practice?

As You Finish This Unit . . .

Take a moment to thank the Lord for the Sermon on the Mount and pray for the Holy Spirit to give you clear understanding, sincere engagement, and wisdom for applying this sermon to your life. Pray for others who may engage this study at the same time as you. Also, while each week focuses on only one portion of the Sermon on the Mount, consider taking 15–20 minutes each week to reread all of Matthew 5–7.

Definitions

[1] **Kingdom of God** – The rule of God manifested in the long-awaited restoration of his people and indeed the whole world, in which God's people will gladly submit to his good rule. When Jesus came 2,000 years ago, he announced that the kingdom of God had arrived (Mark 1:15; Luke 17:20–21). Yet because of ongoing rebellion and rejection of Jesus and his rule, the kingdom still awaits its final consummation and fulfillment in Jesus' second coming (Mark 14:25).

[2] **New creation** – The world to come, which stands in contrast with this "present evil age" (see Gal. 1:4; 6:15). From the moment humanity alienated itself from God, this present world in all its facets has been corrupted by sin. Christ's resurrection marks the dawn of a new world, a new creation, in which everything will be as it was created to be. Through union with Christ by the Spirit, believers are a first expression of this new creation (2 Cor. 5:17), and, when Christ returns to judge and complete his redeeming work, the entire world will experience its transformation into this new creation.

WEEK 2: THE BEATITUDES

AN INVITATION TO TRUE FLOURISHING

Matthew 5:1–12

The Place of the Passage

Jesus begins the Sermon on the Mount with what we now call the "Beatitudes." Each of these nine statements of Jesus begins with the Greek word *makarios*. The Latin translation of *makarios* is *beatus*, which means "blessed" or "happy" or "flourishing" and is why we call them the Beatitudes. These statements of blessing highlight the countercultural vision of the good life that Jesus is bringing into the world. With each statement Jesus affirms, celebrates, and encourages the way of true flourishing. These blessings communicate the characteristics of the people of his kingdom. The Beatitudes provide a concise picture of both the blessings Jesus brings with his kingdom and the characteristic qualities of those who receive these blessings.

The Big Picture

Jesus pronounces statements of blessing and affirmation on those who demonstrate the characteristics of the members of his kingdom.

> ## Reflection and Discussion

Carefully and thoughtfully read this introductory section to Jesus' Sermon on the Mount, Matthew 5:1–12. Then use the provided questions to help you think more deeply about the text. (See *ESV Study Bible* notes on pages 1827–1828; online at www.esv.org.)

Introduction (Matt. 5:1–2)

Matthew 5 transitions us from what Jesus did (Matt. 4:23–25) to what he said: "And he opened his mouth and taught them" (5:2). Before that statement Matthew describes the setting. First, what is significant about the statement that Jesus "went up on the mountain"? (Look to Ex. 3:1–14; 19:1–20:26 for help with the answer.) Second, what is significant about the statement "he sat down"? (Look to Acts 13:14; 16:13; Heb. 1:3; and Rev. 3:21 for help.) Third, what is significant about the statement "his disciples came to him," and how does this reveal Jesus' original audience?

The Beatitudes (Matt. 5:3–12)

Jesus makes nine statements that describe the "blessed" life. Write down nine words or descriptions of the kind of person or life that your culture generally views as "blessed." Then write down the nine words or phrases Jesus uses to describe those whom he views as truly blessed. How do your two lists differ?

Jesus says that the "kingdom of heaven" (Matt. 5:3, 10) belongs to those who are poor in spirit. "Kingdom of heaven" refers to the reign of God through Jesus, which has broken into the present age and will come in its fullness after he returns. Jesus is promising that those who fit the descriptions in the Beatitudes are those who truly flourish even now and especially in the consummation of the kingdom to come. How can this comfort those who embrace Jesus' values while knowing that such values are out of step with their culture?

Jesus pronounces the first blessing over the "poor in spirit" (Matt. 5:3). We know what it means to be poor in regard to wealth, but what does it mean to be poor in *spirit*? How can you tell if someone is poor in spirit? Consider Psalm 34:18; 51:17; Isaiah 57:15; 66:2.

The second beatitude is Jesus' promise of comfort for those who mourn (Matt. 5:4). Jesus elsewhere claims to fulfill the expectations of Isaiah 61:1–3, which promises an anointed preacher who brings good news (see Luke 4:17–19). In addition to those who mourn, how does Isaiah 61:1–3 describe the people Jesus came to bless? What similarities do you see between Isaiah 61:1–3 and the Beatitudes?

Jesus says that the meek will inherit the earth (Matt. 5:5). Meekness means not timidity but humility. It entails intentional lowliness, gentleness, and servant-heartedness. A meek person does not flaunt his or her strength but harnesses it for good. How would your culture define a successful person? Why would Jesus' promise to the meek surprise many people today?

What does it mean to hunger and thirst for righteousness[1] (Matt. 5:6)? What are two or three things you do, or could start doing, to cultivate this appetite?

The "pure in heart" (v. 8) are those who are "singular"—this is what *pure* means—in their focus and loves. They rightly order their loves and put God above all. What does Jesus promise them, and why is this particularly fitting?

In the Jewish culture of Jesus' day, to call someone a "son" was a statement not only of heritage but of likeness—much like the saying, "like father, like son." Look at Jesus' blessing in verse 9 with this question in mind: What does this imply about what God is like? And then, how does that motivate us to pursue peace with people?

How do verses 10–12 encourage Christians who suffer for identifying with and living for Jesus?

_____

_____

_____

_____

_____

Which beatitude are you most eager to cultivate in your life? What is one practical step you can take, beginning this week, to do so?

_____

_____

_____

_____

_____

Read through the following three sections on *Gospel Glimpses, Whole-Bible Connections*, and *Theological Soundings*. Then take time to consider the *Personal Implications* these sections have for you.

Gospel Glimpses

THE SAVIOR WHO BLESSES. Jesus announces a series of statements that describe the good life—the life that truly flourishes. With each statement he affirms that his people will be blessed. This desire to bless comes from his deepest heart. God has, as the Puritan Richard Sibbes put it, a "spreading goodness." In the beginning he created this wonderful world and blessed humanity. Even after sin and death entered the world, he unfolded his plan to make his blessings flow as "far as the curse is found," as the hymnwriter Isaac Watts put it. God's just judgments are certainly seen in the world and will be experienced by unbelievers forever. Nevertheless, Jesus came to take the curse[2] upon himself at the cross so that he may bless all who will receive him by faith.

COMFORT FOR SINNERS AND SUFFERERS. Jesus blesses those who mourn with the promise of comfort. No matter how deep and piercing our pain, God's comfort penetrates deeper still. All who mourn and look to God will receive the comfort only he can give (2 Cor. 1:3–4). Many of us grieve the loss of family or dear friends. We mourn our own sin and its damaging effects. We grieve the injustices in this world. Jesus is not aloof from any of this; he sees it all and promises to bring eternal comfort to his people.

Whole-Bible Connections

MOUNTAINS. Mountains are a significant theme in the Bible. Eden was a mountain sanctuary, Noah's ark rested on a mountain, God covenanted with Israel at Mount Sinai, David reigned from Mount Zion (which was also where Solomon built the temple), and Isaiah promised that God would serve a great eschatological feast for all nations on a mountain (Isa. 25:6). Mountains were also the locations of Jesus' miraculous feedings, his radiant transfiguration,[3] and the great commission to his disciples. Mountains are symbolic connection-places between heaven and earth; they are places of significance and revelation. Jesus highlighted the historical significance of his teaching by ascending a mountain to deliver the message that is the subject of our study.

THE KINGDOM OF HEAVEN. The primary blessing Jesus pronounces in the Beatitudes is the "kingdom of heaven." This term sums up the great blessings Jesus is bringing into the world, all of which lead ultimately to the renewal of the whole creation. We first see God's kingdom in Eden, where God's people enjoy his presence and reflect his rule. When sin entered the world, humanity was sent away from his presence and no longer reflected his rule. Yet God began unfolding his plan to reestablish his kingdom in the world. A major step in this plan was Israel's kingdom and the Davidic king who ruled over them. As historically wonderful as this was, the prophets demonstrated that this was a symbolic picture anticipating a greater kingdom to come; the prophets foresaw a new creation in which God's people would once again enjoy his presence. Jesus arrived and proclaimed the good news of this kingdom's arrival in the middle of history. The kingdom has already dawned, and we await its full consummation after Jesus' return.

COMFORT. God's message throughout the Bible is that he loves to bring comfort to sinners and sufferers through Jesus. After Israel had rejected God for centuries and then experienced exile from their land, God announced the promise of his coming kingdom with these words: "Comfort, comfort my people, says your God" (Isa. 40:1). God promised to send an anointed preacher to "comfort all who mourn" (Isa. 61:2). Centuries later a man named Simeon was "waiting for the consolation of Israel" (Luke 2:25). When Jesus was born, Simeon took him in his arms and rejoiced that the Comforter had come. Jesus bore on the cross the discomfort of eternal judgment, he sent his Spirit as our Comforter, and he will return to end all mourning as God will wipe every tear from our eyes (Rev. 21:4).

Theological Soundings

ESCHATOLOGICAL BLESSING. Jesus promises that his people will ("they shall," used six times in the Beatitudes) experience the blessings of the kingdom of heaven: inheriting the earth, being comforted, seeing God, and so forth. These are "eschatological,"[4] or end-time, blessings. They will be experienced fully in the age to come, the time of the resurrection and the new creation. Even though we wait for the consummation of these blessings in the future, we experience them even now since Jesus has launched his kingdom in this present age.

THE PERSECUTED CHURCH. One of the sad realities of this age is that, as Jesus' people live in faith and love, they will experience persecution (Matt. 5:10–12). Jesus taught Christians to expect the same mistreatment the prophets experienced (v. 12). This means that throughout history we can expect Jesus' church to be a persecuted church. Jesus never taught his people to expect perfect health, cultural acceptance, or abundant wealth in this age. He taught us to expect persecution, not prosperity. Even so, his persecuted people are truly blessed, for theirs is the kingdom of heaven.

Personal Implications

Reflect on how to apply what you have learned in this text to your everyday life. Make notes below on personal implications of (1) the *Gospel Glimpses*, (2) the *Whole-Bible Connections*, (3) the *Theological Soundings*, and (4) this passage as a whole. Also write down what you have learned that can lead you to praise God, repent of sin, trust his gracious promises, and live in obedience to him.

1. Gospel Glimpses

2. Whole-Bible Connections

3. Theological Soundings

----

4. Matthew 5:1–12

> ### As You Finish This Unit . . .

Take a moment to pray and ask for the Lord's blessing and help as you continue in this study of Matthew 5:1–12. And take a moment also to look back through this unit of study, to reflect on a few key things that the Lord may be teaching you—and perhaps to highlight and underline these things to review again in the future.

Definitions

[1] **Righteousness** – The quality of being morally right and without sin—one of God's distinctive attributes. God imputes righteousness to (i.e., he justifies) those who trust in Jesus Christ. "Unrighteousness" describes the absence of righteousness, or behavior contrary to righteousness.

[2] **The curse** – In response to Adam and Eve's rebellion against him, God cursed Satan, humanity, and the entire creation (Gen. 3:14–19). Yet God also promised to bring blessing back to the world, thus reversing the curse and restoring the original blessing of creation (Gen. 3:15; 12:1–3). Through the death and resurrection of Jesus, these promises have begun to be fulfilled. The ultimate fulfillment of these promises is still to come.

[3] **Transfiguration** – An event in the life of Jesus Christ in which his physical appearance was transfigured, that is, changed to reflect his heavenly glory (see Matt. 17:1–13).

[4] **Eschatology** – Study of the events that will occur in the "last days," including a time of tribulation, the return of Christ, the resurrection of humanity, divine judgment, the casting into hell of unrepentant sinners, and the everlasting joy in the new creation for those who trust Jesus. Eschatology, as the word is now used, also has to do with how these end-time realities have broken into the world with the reign of Christ, which began with his first coming.

WEEK 3: FAITHFUL WITNESS AND THE FULFILLMENT OF SCRIPTURE

Matthew 5:13–20

▲

The Place of the Passage

Jesus began the Sermon on the Mount with his nine Beatitudes. These hopeful statements affirmed and celebrated those who live the truly good life—the life that leads to flourishing in God's kingdom now and forever. In this transitional section of Matthew 5:13–20 Jesus brings the Beatitudes to a conclusion by encouraging his disciples to live as faithful witnesses in the world. He calls his disciples to this life of good works by use of the metaphors of salt and light. Jesus also introduces the next section of his teaching by affirming that he has come not to abolish the law[1] or the prophets[2] but to fulfill them.

The Big Picture

Jesus concludes the Beatitudes by encouraging his disciples to live as salt and light in the world, and he introduces his identity as the one who came to fulfill the Old Testament.

> ### Reflection and Discussion

Carefully and thoughtfully read this section of the Sermon on the Mount, Matthew 5:13–20. Then use the provided questions to help you think more deeply about the text. (See *ESV Study Bible* notes on pages 1828–1829; online at www.esv.org.)

Faithful Witness: Living as Salt and Light in the World (5:13–16)

The first-century world used salt for many purposes: as a flavor enhancer, as a preservative, and in covenant-making settings to symbolize the permanence of an agreement. Although it is not clear which specific purpose of salt is in view here, in each case salt has a positive influence in the world. Jesus will soon clarify that this positive influence consists of good works. What are a few ways in which Christians can act as salt in their neighborhoods, workplaces, and broader culture?

What are some ways that Christians can lose their "saltiness" and become ineffective witnesses for Christ in society (Matt. 5:13)?

Jesus says Christians are the "light of the world" (Matt. 5:14). Just before the Sermon on the Mount, in Matthew 4:15–16 Jesus quoted Isaiah 9:2 to describe his ministry: "The people dwelling in darkness have seen a great light, and for those dwelling in the region and shadow of death, on them a light has dawned" (see also Isa. 42:6–7; 49:6). Jesus is the true light of the world, yet he calls his followers to continue this sacred mission. How do Christians continue Jesus' light-shining ministry in the world today?

What specifically does Jesus say we are to do in order to shine as light (see Matt. 5:14–16)? Describe an example you have seen of a Christian doing this well.

What ultimate reason does Jesus give for why we should produce good works (Matt. 5:16)? How do our lives of good works, paired with the sharing of the good news about Jesus, ultimately lead people to glorify God?

How do the characteristics in the Beatitudes (vv. 3–12) help us understand what it looks like to live as salt and light? Which of the characteristics from the Beatitudes do you think is most urgent for Christians to express in our culture today?

The Fulfillment of Scripture (Matt. 5:17–20)

Jesus uses the phrase "the Law and the Prophets" to summarize the entire Old Testament (Matt. 5:17; see 7:12; 11:13; 22:40; Luke 24:27, 44). Jesus did not come to abolish the Old Testament Scriptures, but neither did he come merely to "teach," "keep," or "reinstate" them; he came to "fulfill" them. This means Jesus is that to which the Old Testament was pointing, with all of its commands, promises, and overarching storyline. What are a few ways in which Jesus brings the Old Testament to fulfillment?

Some people think that, because Jesus saves us by grace, it is not important for Christians to pursue good works seriously. How do Jesus' words in Matthew 5:18–19 differ from that view?

The scribes[4] and Pharisees[5] were Jewish leaders who devoted their whole lives to obedience, yet Jesus expects his people to surpass their righteousness (Matt. 5:20)! What do we learn about these leaders' "righteousness" from Matthew 15:7–9; 23:1–33? In light of this, how would you describe the different kind of righteousness for which Jesus calls?

Although Jesus does not require sinless obedience here, he is still calling for a new, radical, inwardly produced kind of righteous living. We may wonder how he can expect us actually to live this way. The key is understanding that Jesus is inaugurating the long-promised new covenant.[5] Read and note what you learn from the central new-covenant promises of Jeremiah 31:31–33 and Ezekiel 36:26–27. How do these promises give you hope for moral transformation?

Some people claim that the Old Testament is no longer important for Christians. They believe it is irrelevant for helping people know Jesus and that Christians should leave it behind. How should we respond to such claims in light of Matthew 5:17–20?

Read through the following three sections on *Gospel Glimpses, Whole-Bible Connections*, and *Theological Soundings*. Then take time to consider the *Personal Implications* these sections have for you.

Gospel Glimpses

A NEW IDENTITY. Jesus does not merely tell people to start pursuing good works; he first calls them to embrace a new identity. He always says "you are" before saying "do this." Jesus does not call us to live moral lives or to love in order to earn a place in his kingdom. No, he first reminds us of our identity as his followers: We *are* the salt of the earth. We *are* the light of the word. It is not about what we do; it is a new identity that we receive as a gift. Only when we embrace this new identity in Christ can we then live it out. What a relief! We do not obey to become Christ's; we obey because we are already his.

A NEW RIGHTEOUSNESS. Jesus calls his people to a righteousness greater than that of the professional law-teachers of his day. We may wonder if he is serious. Perhaps he simply wants us to despair so that we see our need of forgiveness. Three keys help us understand his meaning. First, it is true that we cannot obey on our own. Jesus alone obeys perfectly, and he came to die in our place so that we could be forgiven. Second, he is calling us not to a greater *amount* of righteousness but to a different *kind* of righteousness—a sincere obedience from the heart, unlike the hypocritical Pharisees' cheaply manufactured and hollow morality. Third, Jesus has inaugurated his kingdom, and with it the promises of the new covenant, which includes new hearts and Spirit-produced transformation (Jer. 31:31–34; Ezek. 36:27). Jesus calls us to sincere obedience, but he also provides both forgiveness for our failures and empowerment by his Spirit.

Whole-Bible Connections

THE FULFILLMENT OF THE LAW. Jesus said he came not to abolish the law and the prophets but to fulfill them. He said elsewhere that the law and the prophets as a whole were prophetic: "All the Prophets and the Law prophesied until John [the Baptist]" (Matt. 11:13). The whole Old Testament—from its commands to its covenantal structure—pointed prophetically to the arrival of Jesus and his kingdom. Jesus does not merely fulfill a few scattered predictions; he brings the entirety of the Scriptures to their appointed goal. The Old Testament was an arrow, with Jesus as its tip. With his kingdom he brought in the new age that fulfills every ancient promise. He is the long-awaited prophet, priest, and king. He is the true temple of God's presence and the final sacrifice for sins. He inaugurated the new covenant and launched the new creation. Now he generously pours out the promised Spirit to create new hearts in a new humanity that must live with glad-hearted obedience.

THE LIGHT OF THE WORLD. When Jesus calls his people the "light of the world" (Matt. 5:14), he echoes an ancient theme from the prophet Isaiah. In Isaiah 42:6 God said Israel was to be his servant and a "light for the nations." Israel failed in this calling, so a new and better Servant, a true Israel, a singular Savior would come both to restore Israel and to be the true "light for the nations" (Isa. 49:6). When Jesus came, he announced himself to be this long-awaited Servant: "I am the light of the world" (John 8:12). He beautifully fulfills Israel's calling to shine as light in the dark world. And, when he shines on us, we come out of darkness and into his marvelous light (Col. 1:13; 1 Pet. 2:9). Now all who are transformed by his light receive this new identity and mission: to join him in fulfilling Israel's calling as the "light of the world" (Matt. 5:14)

Theological Soundings

GOOD WORKS. Jesus calls us to shine brightly with kindness so that people "may see your good works and give glory to your Father who is in heaven" (Matt. 5:16). The Bible is clear: we are not saved *by* good works, but we are nevertheless saved *for* good works. As Ephesians 2:9–10 says, although our salvation is "not a result of works," we are nevertheless "created in Christ Jesus *for* good works." Jesus, the only one to ever live a perfect life, died a "guilty" death in order to forgive all our sins. But he also rose again and poured out his Spirit to create a new humanity, eager to become like him. He did this to "purify for himself a people for his own possession who are zealous for good works" (Titus 2:14). This is what it means to be a disciple: to learn from Jesus and to become like him by the power of the Holy Spirit. As we shine with good works, people will see God's power and perhaps be drawn to trust and glorify him.

Personal Implications

Reflect on how to apply what you have learned in this text to your everyday life. Make notes below on personal implications of (1) the *Gospel Glimpses*, (2) the *Whole-Bible Connections*, (3) the *Theological Soundings*, and (4) this passage as a whole. Also write down what you have learned that can lead you to praise God, repent of sin, trust his gracious promises, and live in obedience to him.

1. Gospel Glimpses

2. Whole-Bible Connections

3. Theological Soundings

4. Matthew 5:13–20

> ## As You Finish This Unit . . .

Take a moment to pray and ask for the Lord's blessing and help as you continue in this study of Matthew 5:13–20. And take a moment also to look back through this unit of study, to reflect on a few key things that the Lord may be teaching you—and perhaps to highlight and underline these things to review again in the future.

Definitions

[1] **Law** – When spelled with an initial capital letter, "Law" refers to the first five books of the Bible. The Law contains numerous commands of God to his people, including the Ten Commandments and instructions regarding worship, sacrifice, and life in Israel. The NT often uses "the law" (lower case) to refer to the entire body of precepts set forth in the books of the Law.

[2] **Prophet** – Someone who speaks authoritatively for God. When the NT refers to "the prophets," it is referring either to a specific group of OT books ("the Prophets," with an initial capital letter, e.g., Matt. 5:17; Luke 24:44) or, more generally, to those who spoke to God's people on behalf of God throughout the OT between the time of Moses and the close of the OT (lower case, "the prophets," e.g., Matt. 16:14; Acts 15:15).

[3] **Scribe** – Someone trained and authorized to transcribe, teach, and interpret the Scriptures. Jesus often criticized the scribes for their pride, their legalistic approach to the Scriptures, and their refusal to believe in him.

[4] **Pharisees** – A popular religious/political party in NT times characterized by strict adherence to the law of Moses and also to extrabiblical Jewish traditions. The Pharisees were frequently criticized by Jesus for their legalistic and hypocritical practices.

[5] **New covenant** – Covenant prophesied in Jeremiah 31:31–34 and established through the death and resurrection of Christ. In this covenant, those who place their faith in Christ are forgiven through his atoning work, and these believers are enabled to remain faithful to God henceforth through the law's being "written on their hearts" by the Holy Spirit.

WEEK 4: TRUE RIGHTEOUSNESS

PART 1: ANGER AND LUST

Matthew 5:21–30

▲

The Place of the Passage

In the first part of the Sermon on the Mount Jesus made several short state-ments clarifying the truly blessed, happy, and flourishing life. Then he called his disciples to live as salt and light in the world—to live influential lives of good works for the common good and the glory of God. He also said he did not come to abolish the Scriptures but to bring them to their intended goal in himself. Now that his kingdom has dawned, his people must have a truer and deeper righteousness than that of the hypocritical scribes and Pharisees. Jesus now explains what this "greater righteousness" looks like in six different realms. Here we consider the first two: anger and lust. Jesus contrasts what his hearers were previously taught with his kingdom's new standard of righteousness.

The Big Picture

Jesus contrasts what people previously heard from the scribes and Pharisees regarding anger and lust with the new standards of his kingdom.

> ## Reflection and Discussion

Carefully and thoughtfully read this section of Jesus' teaching, Matthew 5:21–30. Then use the provided questions to help you think more deeply about the text. (See *ESV Study Bible* notes on page 1829; online at www.esv.org.)

Instruction about Anger (Matt. 5:21–26)

Jesus introduces each new topic in the rest of Matthew 5 with the words "you have heard that it was said" or "it was said" (vv. 21, 27, 31, 33, 38, 43). Where did Jesus' original audience hear these ethical teachings before—from the OT, the moral Jewish tradition, or a mixture of the two? Why would it have been shocking for Jesus' audience to hear him add after each one, "but I say to you . . ." (vv. 22, 28, 32, 34, 39, 44)? What does this show us about the identity of Jesus?

Jesus has just said that he came not to abolish the law and the prophets but to fulfill them (Matt. 5:17). One way he brings the law to fulfillment is by showing God's deeper and higher standards for his new-covenant people, whom he will empower by giving them new hearts and the Holy Spirit. In light of this, how does the old-covenant command not to murder relate to Jesus' command not to be angry (vv. 21–22)?

Read Ephesians 4:26 (cf. Ps. 4:4) and consider, Is it always wrong to be angry? If not, what is the difference between righteous and unrighteous anger?

Note how Jesus describes the urgency of reconciliation[1] in Matthew 5:23–26. Why is reconciliation in relationships so vital?

Read Colossians 3:13. How does this verse demonstrate Jesus' teaching on reconciliation? How does it also show us the way we can be motivated and empowered to pursue reconciliation?

Instruction about Lust (Matt. 5:27–30)

Jesus brings the old-covenant[2] command against adultery to fulfillment by showing how lust is already adultery in the heart (Matt. 5:27–28). How is lust related to adultery?

Think through Jesus' reasoning and motivation here and answer this question in light of them: Why is lust both wrong and foolish?

Jesus says to tear out one's eye or to cut off one's hand if they cause one to lust (Matt. 5:29–30). Neither action would actually prevent someone from lusting, since lust is a sin of the heart. What, then, is Jesus' point?

The New Testament is clear that no amount of good works or sin prevention will earn our salvation. Salvation is by grace alone, through faith alone, in Christ alone (see Eph. 2:1–10). Yet Jesus urges us to fight the sin of lust, "for it is better that you lose one of your members than that your whole body be thrown into hell" (Matt. 5:29–30). How do we reconcile the gracious reality of salvation with the necessity of fighting sin?

What radical and practical steps might you need to take in order to fight against lust?

Read through the following three sections on *Gospel Glimpses, Whole-Bible Connections*, and *Theological Soundings*. Then take time to consider the *Personal Implications* these sections have for you.

Gospel Glimpses

THE DOUBLE CURE OF FORGIVENESS AND TRANSFORMATION. Jesus calls his people to a beautiful standard of peacemaking and purity in place of anger and lust. He clearly expects us to pursue these standards, and yet we must remember: he gives this teaching on the way to his cross and resurrection. It is through his dying and rising again that Jesus inaugurates the new covenant, regarding which the prophet Jeremiah promised not only complete forgiveness[3] but also ethical transformation and power (Matt. 26:26–28; see Jer. 31:31–34). Cleansing and renewal together make up the double cure we need in order to pursue Jesus' standards. When we hear his standards, we must always (1) receive his forgiveness for our failures and (2) rely on the Holy Spirit's transforming power.

A WORLD WITHOUT ANGER. Jesus' teaching on anger serves not just as an urgent ethical standard but also as a hopeful glimpse of the world to come. Jesus is showing the ethical beauty of the community he creates through his kingdom. Since the kingdom has already dawned, those who follow Jesus can and will live according to his standards, though certainly not perfectly. But this is our great hope: when the kingdom comes in all its fullness, it will give way to a new creation, in which the Lord's people will fulfill his standards perfectly. The new creation will be a world without murder, anger, or strife. It will be a world of perfect peace and joyful harmony. Jesus' commands ultimately turn our gaze to the horizon of his return, when all will be set right.

Whole-Bible Connections

FULFILLMENT OF THE LAW. Jesus' instruction on anger and lust come in the context of his claim to fulfill the law and the prophets (Matt. 5:17). He did not come merely to clarify or to reinforce the law. If he had done so, he would have merely unpacked and explained what it meant not to murder or commit adultery. Instead, he calls his people not just to avoid murder but to avoid getting angry. He calls them not just to avoid adultery but to avoid lust. Jesus is bringing the Old Testament commands to fulfillment in himself. The murder and adultery commands are part of the Scriptures that prophetically anticipate the new-covenant era, in which Jesus brings a deeper, heart-rooted, holistic obedience. In light of this, the command not to murder is fulfilled in God's people as they renounce unrighteous anger (5:21–26). The command against adultery is fulfilled as they renounce even lustful thoughts (5:27–30). Each command is caught up in the bigger story of the Bible that finds its fulfillment in Jesus' kingdom and the heart-level transformation he brings.

Theological Soundings

THE AUTHORITY OF JESUS. Six times in Matthew 5 Jesus says something like, "You have heard that it was said . . . but I say to you . . ." (Matt. 5:21–22, 27–28, 31–32, 33–34, 38–39, 43–44). Jesus contrasts what his disciples had heard and been taught (both in the Old Testament and from teachers of the law) with his own instruction. Jesus therefore demonstrates that he is the ultimate authority to whom people must now look. Jesus is not just a good man and a great ethical teacher; he is the divine Son of God to whom people from every nation must submit.

SIN AND THE HEART. Jesus repeatedly emphasizes that the ethical standards of his kingdom cannot be met by mere external obedience. It is not enough to avoid murder; Jesus condemns anger and insults and calls us to pursue true reconciliation (Matt. 5:21–24). It is not enough to avoid adultery; Jesus says that looking at someone with lustful intent is already adultery committed in the heart (vv. 27–28). Jesus teaches elsewhere that "Out of the heart come evil thoughts, murder, adultery, sexual immorality, theft, false witness, slander" (15:19). Sin is not just what we do; it flows from the inside out.

JUDGMENT AND HELL. As Jesus addresses the sins of anger and lust, he speaks about people's being "liable to the hell of fire" (Matt. 5:22) and their bodies' being "thrown into hell" (5:29). Jesus draws attention to the eternal consequences of sin. Humanity's sins, such as anger and lust, are harmful to others, are offensive to God, and warrant eternal judgment. All those who refuse forgiveness through Christ will one day stand before him to hear the sentence of eternal death. But let us not misunderstand: The fact that Jesus spoke about judgment does not diminish his love; it demonstrates it. He warned about hell because he did not want people to experience it. Indeed, when he spoke of hell he was also speaking of what he would experience on the cross in the place of sinners like us who deserve to go there.

Personal Implications

Reflect on how to apply what you have learned in this text to your everyday life. Make notes below on personal implications of (1) the *Gospel Glimpses*, (2) the

Whole-Bible Connections, (3) the *Theological Soundings*, and (4) this passage as a whole. Also write down what you have learned that can lead you to praise God, repent of sin, trust his gracious promises, and live in obedience to him.

1. Gospel Glimpses

2. Whole-Bible Connections

3. Theological Soundings

4. Matthew 5:21–30

As You Finish This Unit . . .

Take a moment to pray and ask for the Lord's blessing and help as you continue in this study of Matthew 5:21–30. And take a moment also to look back through this unit of study, to reflect on a few key things that the Lord may be teaching you—and perhaps to highlight and underline these things to review again in the future.

Definitions

[1] **Reconciliation** – The restoration of a positive relationship and peace between alienated or opposing parties. Through his death and resurrection, Jesus has reconciled believers to God (2 Cor. 5:18–21).

[2] **Covenant** – A binding agreement between two parties, typically involving a formal statement of their relationship, a list of stipulations and obligations for both parties, a list of witnesses to the agreement, and a list of curses for unfaithfulness and blessings for faithfulness to the agreement. The OT is more properly understood as the old covenant, meaning the agreement established between God and his people prior to the coming of Jesus Christ and the establishment of the new covenant.

[3] **Forgiveness** – Release from guilt and the reestablishment of relationship. Forgiveness can be granted by God to human beings (Luke 24:47; 1 John 1:9) and by human beings to those who have wronged them (Matt. 18:21–22; Col. 3:13).

WEEK 5: TRUE RIGHTEOUSNESS

PART 2: DIVORCE AND OATHS

Matthew 5:31–37

▲

The Place of the Passage

Jesus has launched his kingdom and with it has brought the law and the prophets to fulfillment. He now calls his disciples to live as the light of the world, which will entail living out his kingdom's ethical standards. In particular, his people must have a heart-rooted and whole-life righteousness, which is entirely different than the righteousness of the scribes and Pharisees. Jesus offers six examples of what this greater righteousness looks like. Having instructed his disciples regarding the first two, anger and lust, Jesus now turns to divorce and oaths.

The Big Picture

Jesus contrasts what people have heard about divorce and oaths with the new standards of his kingdom.

> ## Reflection and Discussion

Carefully and thoughtfully read this section of Jesus' teaching, Matthew 5:31–37. Then use the provided questions to help you think more deeply about the text. (See *ESV Study Bible* notes on pages 1829–1830; online at www.esv.org.)

Instruction about Divorce (Matt. 5:31–32)

Read Moses' instructions about divorce in Deuteronomy 24:1–4. Summarize what Jesus now teaches in response to this.

Read Jesus' expanded teaching on divorce in Matthew 19:1–12. Notice that Jesus appeals to God's original intention for marriage from Genesis 1–2 before explaining his view of divorce. How does Jesus summarize God's original design for marriage? Why is it important to understand God's design for marriage before we consider any potential allowance for divorce?

Jesus says he does not permit divorce except in the case of "sexual immorality" (Matt. 5:32; 19:9). What constitutes "sexual immorality"? Why does Jesus single out such sin as potentially covenant-breaking?

While Jesus mentions only the exception of sexual immorality for divorce, the apostle Paul notes one more scenario as a potential ground for divorce. Summarize in your own words what Paul teaches in 1 Corinthians 7:13–15. Do you think, based on those two exceptions, that there are any other acceptable reasons for divorce?

How would you summarize your culture's general view on marriage and divorce? What are a few ways in which Jesus' vision differs?

What can currently married men and women do to cultivate faithfulness in marriage? What might repentance to God and a spouse look like for someone who has failed to uphold Jesus' standard at this point? Is there a particular step you need to take in light of these reflections?

Instruction about Oaths (Matt. 5:33–37)

Jesus summarizes what the disciples knew about oaths from the Old Testament: "You shall not swear falsely, but shall perform to the Lord what you have sworn"

(Matt. 5:33). Summarize what each of these Old Testament texts teaches about oaths: Leviticus 19:11–12; Numbers 30:2; and Deuteronomy 23:21–23.

God's original, noble design for human speech is that it be marked by straight-forward truth-telling. God's law for Israel allowed and gave instructions for oaths. However, in the first century AD it was common to swear by any number of holy objects (see Matt. 23:16–21). It was also common to attempt to get out of following through on one's oaths. How does Jesus' teaching on truth-telling in Matthew 5:34–37 get to the heart of the matter?

How does Jesus' heart-level and holistic instruction on speech make numerous and elaborate oaths unnecessary?

Read through the following three sections on *Gospel Glimpses, Whole-Bible Connections,* and *Theological Soundings.* Then take time to consider the *Personal Implications* these sections have for you.

Gospel Glimpses

FAITHFUL TO HIS WORD. Jesus calls his people to forgo elaborate or numerous oaths and instead to say simply "yes" or "no" (Matt. 5:37). This calls us to honesty, candor, and faithfulness in our words. This is important to Jesus because this is what he is like, and what his Father is like (see v. 48). We do not need to wonder if God will try to get out of his commitments; he makes promises and keeps them. As 2 Corinthians 1:20 exults, "All the promises of God find their Yes in [Jesus]." God will keep his promise to save all who come to him through Jesus in faith. And God will keep his promise to work everything together for good for those who love him (Rom. 8:28). His "yes" is "yes." He is faithful to his word (see 2 Tim. 2:13).

MARRIAGE AND THE GOSPEL. One reason Jesus urges faithfulness to marriage covenants is because of the ultimate significance of marriage. Marriage itself pictures the union of Christ and his church (Eph. 5:22–33; see 1 Cor. 6:13–19; Rev. 21:1–5). Paul teaches that God designed marriage to point to Christ and the church all along. Speaking of God's original institution of marriage in Eden, Paul writes, "This mystery is profound, and I am saying that it refers to Christ and the church" (Eph. 5:32). At the heart of the gospel[1] is Christ's love for his church, which is his bride. Yet Christ's love runs deeper than the love of anyone else, for he sacrificed his life for us, taking our eternal judgment upon himself so that we might enjoy his kindness forever: "Christ loved the church and gave himself up for her, that he might sanctify her, having cleansed her by the washing of water with the word" (vv. 25b–26). Marriage matters, and faithfulness in marriage matters, because it pictures this strong and beautiful gospel reality.

Whole-Bible Connections

MARRIAGE AND DIVORCE. Jesus quotes Moses' instruction from Deuteronomy 24:1–4, which requires a man who divorces his wife to give her a certificate of divorce. Jesus, however, now says that no one is permitted to divorce a spouse except for sexual immorality. As he expands on this teaching in Matthew 19:1–12, Jesus shows how the ethics of marriage and divorce make sense only in light of the whole story of the Bible. God set the standard in Genesis 1–2 as he established marriage as a lifelong covenant between one man and one woman. After sin entered the world and divorce became prevalent, Moses merely regulated and allowed for it due to the hardness of human hearts (Matt. 19:8). Now that Jesus is bringing his kingdom and the new covenant, however, he reestablishes God's creational design for marriage as a lifelong union not to be severed by casual divorce.

Theological Soundings

THE SIGNIFICANCE OF SPEECH. Jesus selects the topic of oath-making as a primary example of his kingdom's ethics (Matt. 5:33–37). This assumes that our speech matters, perhaps more than we realize (see 12:37). The theological reason why words matter is that we are image-bearers[2] of a communicative God. Humans have unique linguistic capabilities, and our speech is itself a certain kind of action, a speech-action. Words do not just convey information; they affect things. As Proverbs says, "death and life are in the power of the tongue" (Prov. 18:21). In Jesus' example, our word is our bond. We commit ourselves to future actions with our promises. To say simply "yes" or "no," as Jesus commands, is to embrace the theological, practical, and ethical significance of speech.

Personal Implications

Reflect on how to apply what you have learned in this text to your everyday life. Make notes below on personal implications of (1) the *Gospel Glimpses*, (2) the *Whole-Bible Connections*, (3) the *Theological Soundings*, and (4) this passage as a whole. Also write down what you have learned that can lead you to praise God, repent of sin, trust his gracious promises, and live in obedience to him.

1. Gospel Glimpses

2. Whole-Bible Connections

3. Theological Soundings

4. Matthew 5:31–37

> ### As You Finish This Unit . . .

Take a moment to pray and ask for the Lord's blessing and help as you continue in this study of Matthew 5:31–37. And take a moment also to look back through this unit of study, to reflect on a few key things that the Lord may be teaching you—and perhaps to highlight and underline these things to review again in the future.

Definitions

[1] **Gospel** – A common translation for a Greek word meaning "good news," that is, the good news of Jesus Christ and the salvation he made possible by his crucifixion, burial, and resurrection.

[2] **Image-bearer** – The Bible's opening pages ring with the truth that God created humans "in his image" to know and reflect him on earth (Gen. 1:26–27). Just as kings in ancient times would set up statues or "images" on the highest peaks to display their fame and rule, we too are designed to draw attention to our Maker. Though God's image in man was fractured at the fall (Genesis 3), it has not been eradicated. Jesus is the full image of the invisible God (2 Cor. 4:4; Col. 1:15; Heb. 1:3), and in Christians this image is being restored (Rom. 8:29; Eph. 4:24; Col. 3:10).

Week 6: True Righteousness

Part 3: Retaliation and Love

Matthew 5:38–48

The Place of the Passage

The introduction to the Sermon on the Mount showed Jesus' agenda: he is unfolding a countercultural vision of the good life. This is the flourishing life of his kingdom, in which we experience true happiness. He concluded this introduction by affirming that the people of his kingdom are the salt and light of the world. Jesus introduced the next section by affirming that he came not to abolish the Old Testament but to fulfill it. He now demonstrates this by showing how he fulfills the Old Testament in relation to six ethical expectations. The first four have addressed laws about murder, adultery, divorce, and oaths. This section now continues Jesus' explanation with the examples of retaliation and love. In each case we see how Jesus fulfills the law and how we are to live as his disciples in his countercultural kingdom.

The Big Picture

Jesus contrasts what people have heard about retaliation and how to treat enemies with the new standards of his kingdom.

> ## Reflection and Discussion

Carefully and thoughtfully read this section of Jesus' teaching, Matthew 5:38–48. Then use the provided questions to help you think more deeply about the text. (See *ESV Study Bible* notes on pages 1830–1831; online at www.esv.org.)

Instruction about Retaliation (Matt. 5:38–42)

Jesus in Matthew 5:38 draws on Old Testament teaching about judicial retribution. Read the following texts and summarize their teaching on this topic: Exodus 21:24; Leviticus 24:19–20; Deuteronomy 19:21.

Some think that the Old Testament's teaching on judicial retribution encouraged revenge. However, in a world filled with a back-and-forth escalation of vengeful retaliation, how would the Old Testament laws actually limit and neutralize such feuds?

The Old Testament law rightly valued neutralizing feuds by enforcing judicial retribution. How does Jesus' radical teaching in Matthew 5:40–42 go beyond neutralizing hostilities?

Jesus offers four examples in Matthew 5:39–41 of how his teaching on non-retaliation is not an abrogation of the law but a fulfillment of it. His point is not that we must follow these examples in a literalistic, unwise fashion but that we must apply their wisdom to our own circumstances. How would you summarize the main point of these examples? What are a few examples you can think of for how to apply this main point today?

Instruction about Love (Matt. 5:43–47)

The commandment to love one's neighbor echoes Old Testament law (Lev. 19:18); the additional command to "hate your enemy" is an oral tradition that was introduced in Jesus' day and likely came from a misunderstanding and misappropriation of examples in the Old Testament about enemies of God and Israel. How does Jesus not only correct this misunderstanding but point to a deeper and more expansive understanding of what it means to love (Matt. 5:43–44)?

How does God the Father exemplify blessing those who are evil (Matt. 5:45)? What does this teach us about God's character?

As you consider how to apply Matthew 5:43–47 to your life, for whom do you need to start praying, and how can you concretely bless him or her?

_____

_____

_____

_____

_____

This focus on love summarizes fittingly everything Jesus has taught so far. What similarities do you see between Jesus' teaching on love in Matthew 5:43–45 and in the opening sections of the sermon (vv. 3–16)?

_____

_____

_____

_____

_____

_____

Summary of the Ethics of Jesus' Kingdom (Matt. 5:48)

Matthew 5:48 concludes not only the previous section on love (vv. 43–47) but the whole section of verses 17–47. The word "perfect" here refers not to moral perfection but to a sense of holiness[1] and wholeness in one's character; the focus here is especially on indiscriminate love for all people. How does this idea serve as a good summary of the kind of life to which Jesus has called his people so far in the Sermon on the Mount?

_____

_____

_____

_____

_____

_____

Jesus summarizes the ethics of his kingdom with a call to reflect God the Father's own character. How do God's actions throughout redemptive history[2] show him to be the truest embodiment of the virtues to which Jesus calls us in Matthew 5:17–47? Provide a few examples.

How will Jesus go on from here to show the world that he is the ultimate example of the character traits he has taught in this section?

Read through the following three sections on *Gospel Glimpses, Whole-Bible Connections*, and *Theological Soundings*. Then take time to consider the *Personal Implications* these sections have for you.

Gospel Glimpses

A COUNTERCULTURE OF BLESSING. The fallen human heart shamefully escalates feuds by repaying harm sevenfold (see Gen. 4:24). The Old Testament law wisely neutralized feuds by requiring equal repayment—an eye for an eye, a tooth for a tooth. But Jesus brings a new power to create a new, radical standard: give more than what is asked for, love your enemies, and pray for those who curse you. In other words, we can see a progression from our natural instinct to the Old Testament law and to Jesus' new standard: (1) We naturally want to repay *more* than the harm done to us. (2) The Old Testament limits repayment to that which is *equal* to the harm done to us. (3) Jesus calls us to do *good* in place of harm. This is a radical standard, but one that Jesus himself models and empowers. He gives eternal life to those who deserve death, he makes his enemies his friends, and he prays for those who crucify him (Luke 23:34). What can we do but be melted by this love and begin treating others as he so kindly treats us? And, as we do, we will begin creating a counterculture of blessing.

THE FATHER'S KINDNESS. Jesus calls us to a radical standard of kindness in the Sermon on the Mount. And yet he summarizes all of this by calling us to be like the heavenly Father (Matt. 5:45, 48). The ethical life that sounds nearly impossible to us is natural to God the Father. This is what he is like. This is his heart. He is faithful to his word, he blesses those who offend him, and he loves his enemies—and he has shown us this faithful and loving heart through giving his only Son for us on the cross. If you want to summarize the ethical life Jesus calls us to, look to the Father's kindness.

Whole-Bible Connections

REFLECTING THE HOLINESS OF GOD. When Jesus calls his people to "be perfect, as your heavenly Father is perfect" (Matt. 5:48), he echoes the Old Testament command to be holy as God is holy (Lev. 20:26; see also Deut. 18:13). When God called his people to be holy, he was calling them to a life set apart and devoted to him. Jesus evokes this idea and expresses it with a similar word, "perfect." This word refers first not to moral perfection but to a sense of holiness and wholeness in character. This is the kind of life wholly set apart and devoted to God. It is the non-hypocritical and straightforward life of integrity, the life that values God above all things and then thinks, speaks, and acts in light of that reality. We must be holy as God is holy, which means we must devote ourselves wholly to him.

Theological Soundings

COMMON GRACE. Jesus points to his Father's character in order to motivate followers to love their enemies. God the Father "makes his sun rise on the evil and on the good, and sends rain on the just and the unjust" (Matt. 5:45). The sun and the rain are two of God's great and vital gifts to humanity. Yet not one person deserves these blessings. Even so, God gives them indiscriminately to all—to God-lovers and God-haters alike. Theologians refer to this reality of God's universal blessing as "common grace," for it is the grace of God that is common to all people, both those who trust him and those who do not.

IMITATING GOD. Jesus' vision of ethics in Matthew 5:38–48 is largely about imitating God. He summarizes it like this: "Be perfect, as your heavenly Father is perfect" (v. 48). To be perfect here refers to a sense of wholeness. It is a whole-person reflection of God's own good character in all of life. This means that Christian behavior is not arbitrary, nor do we look for a standard of goodness outside of God himself. As the apostle Paul later puts it, we are called to be "imitators of God, as beloved children" (Eph. 5:1). Jesus is inviting us into a Spirit-empowered life that reflects the beauty of God's good character.

Personal Implications

Reflect on how to apply what you have learned in this text to your everyday life. Make notes below on personal implications of (1) the *Gospel Glimpses*, (2) the *Whole-Bible Connections*, (3) the *Theological Soundings*, and (4) this passage as a whole. Also write down what you have learned that can lead you to praise God, repent of sin, trust his gracious promises, and live in obedience to him.

1. Gospel Glimpses

2. Whole-Bible Connections

3. Theological Soundings

4. Matthew 5:38–48

As You Finish This Unit . . .

Take a moment to pray and ask for the Lord's blessing and help as you continue in this study of Matthew 5:38–48. And take a moment also to look back through this unit of study, to reflect on a few key things that the Lord may be teaching you—and perhaps to highlight and underline these things to review again in the future.

Definitions

[1] **Holiness** – A quality possessed by something or someone set apart for a special role in relation to God. When applied to God himself, it refers to his utter perfection and complete transcendence over creation. God's people are called to imitate his holiness (Lev. 19:2), which means being set apart from sin and reserved for his purposes.

[2] **Redemptive history** – The progressive unfolding in history of God's plan to redeem his people. God's purposes of redemption become clearer and more developed through his acts in history and through his successive relation to Adam, Noah, Abraham, Moses, David, and the prophets, and in the New Testament.

WEEK 7: A GODWARD LIFE

Matthew 6:1–8

▲

The Place of the Passage

In Matthew 5:17–20 Jesus called his disciples to pursue a "righteousness" that "exceeds," or is greater than, that of the scribes and Pharisees—a righteousness from the heart and through all of life. Jesus illustrated this new standard with six contrasting ethical examples of what this new righteousness looks like (5:21–48). Jesus now continues to explain this true righteousness by focusing on three examples of religious devotion and piety: giving to the needy, prayer, and fasting (6:1–18). Here in verses 1–8 Jesus focuses first on how his disciples must give and pray with sincerity rather than with a desire to be seen and praised by others. This is a vision of a Godward life—a life lived not for the sight and praise of others but for God.

The Big Picture

Jesus' disciples must give and pray not to be seen by others but with sincerity and to be seen and rewarded by God.

Reflection and Discussion

Carefully and thoughtfully read this section of Jesus' teaching, Matthew 6:1–8. Then use the provided questions to help you think more deeply about the text. (See *ESV Study Bible* notes on page 1831; online at www.esv.org.)

Warning about Practicing Righteousness in Order to Be Seen (Matt. 6:1)

Jesus begins this section with a warning: "Beware of practicing your righteousness before other people in order to be seen by them" (Matt. 6:1). What is the deep issue of the heart against which Jesus calls us to guard?

Read Matthew 6:1 and compare it to what Jesus says in 5:16. How does this at first seem like a contradiction? Yet how do these two statements actually complement, rather than contradict, each other? Consider the particular actions and motives in view for each statement.

How does this warning in Matthew 6:1 relate to Jesus' statement in Matthew 5:20?

Giving to Those in Need (Matt. 6:2–4)

Jesus contrasts what his disciples must do with what the "hypocrites" do (Matt. 6:2). What do you learn about the meaning of hypocrisy from Matthew 7:5; 15:7–8; and 23:26–27? How would you summarize what it means to be a hypocrite?

Jesus says that, when hypocrites give to the poor, they "sound a trumpet" in the synagogues and in the streets—both locations where giving would take place (Matt. 6:2). What is their motivation and goal in broadcasting their piety? What are a few ways today by which people "sound a trumpet" when they give?

What does it mean not to let your left hand know what your right is doing when you give (Matt. 6:3)? What is a practical example of what this can look like in your life?

After Jesus warns against a hypocritical desire to be seen for our generosity, we may expect him to say that we should give because it is right, good, or our duty. But what does he use to encourage us in Matthew 6:4, and why might this surprise us?

Praying to the Father (Matt. 6:5–8)

How do the hypocrites in Matthew 6:5 misuse, and miss the point of, prayer?

Matthew 6:6–8 is not so much about the length or frequency of our prayers but about our underlying view of God and our trust in him. What do we learn about the Gentiles' (pagans') view of their God or gods from the way in which they pray?

What do we learn about God from the way in which Jesus encourages us to pray?

Throughout this passage Jesus addresses the danger of intentionally displaying our goodness, piety, or virtue so that others notice and think well of us. What examples of this do you see in your culture's physical or digital public areas?

Read through the following three sections on *Gospel Glimpses, Whole-Bible Connections*, and *Theological Soundings*. Then take time to consider the *Personal Implications* these sections have for you.

Gospel Glimpses

YOUR FATHER. Three times in this short section Jesus draws our attention to God the Father (Matt. 6:1, 4, 6). This is his characteristic way of referring to God throughout the Sermon on the Mount. And yet it is not that Jesus simply draws attention to the fatherhood of God in general. In each case he references not *the* Father but *your* Father. There is gospel-wonder in that little pronoun. There is an infinite difference between knowing that God is *the* Father and knowing him as *your* Father. One of the greatest blessings of the gospel is that those who are united to Jesus by faith are adopted[1] into God's family. As Ephesians 1:5 says, God "predestined us for adoption to himself as sons through Jesus Christ."

GOD SEES YOU. Jesus taps into a deep motivation of the human heart: the desire to be seen and honored. Our problem is not that we want this but that we look for its fulfillment in the wrong places. We seek to be seen and honored by others rather than to be seen and honored by God. This is not merely misguided; it is idolatry.[2] This is also what leads to a hypocritical life of projecting the image of praising God while actually seeking praise from others. But Jesus has come not just to expose this idolatry but graciously to invite us to fulfill this desire in God alone. Jesus does so by drawing attention to God's kindness. God sees every good work done in secret and hears every prayer offered in private, and he will honor us for them. No one else may know, but the one whose opinion really matters does know. We have a God who sees and who delights to bless.

Whole-Bible Connections

GOD LOOKS ON THE HEART. Jesus warns against practicing righteousness in order to be seen by others—sounding a trumpet when we give, praying on street corners to be seen by others, and so forth (Matt. 6:1–8). Jesus calls us instead to heart-rooted righteousness. He calls us to actions that may not be valued by others but that God sees and honors. We see this theme prominently in the narratives contrasting Saul and David in 1 Samuel. The people desire a tall and powerful king like Saul even though he lacks character, but God knows the heart and chooses David. As God tells Samuel when he sends him to anoint David, "Man looks on the outward appearance, but the LORD looks on the heart" (1 Sam. 16:7).

Theological Soundings

REWARDS. Jesus motivates generous giving and sincere praying with the gracious promise of reward. He promises, "Your Father who sees in secret will reward you" (Matt. 6:4; see also vv. 1, 6). This may at first sound like talk of merit and earning. But it is not. Jesus is speaking of rewards. Rewards are the gracious result of embracing and expressing Jesus' teaching. Nothing we do prior to our salvation is worthy of reward, and even after we are saved our good works will still have something in them that needs to be forgiven. So, we always stand in need of God's forgiving grace, and no good thing he gives us is earned or deserved. Nevertheless, his grace is so great that he not only forgives us but he empowers us by his Spirit to do good works—and then he promises to reward them. A day is coming when Jesus will assess our works, commend that which is good, and invite us to "enter into the joy of your master" (Matt. 25:21, 23; see also 1 Cor. 4:5; Heb. 11:6; 1 Pet. 1:6–7). Seeking reward from God is a proper motivation for Christian obedience.

GOD'S OMNISCIENCE. As Jesus encourages his people to practice devotional acts in secret, he motivates them with the truth that "Your Father who sees in secret will reward you" (Matt. 6:4, 6). God sees everything we do because God is omniscient, which means he is all-knowing. As the apostle John puts it, God "knows everything" (1 John 3:20). This is the doctrine of God's omniscience, and it is affirmed throughout the Bible. God knows everything about us, including the very thoughts of our hearts (1 Kings 8:39; 1 Chron. 28:9; Pss. 44:21; 139:1–4; Acts 1:24).

PRAYER AND THE KNOWLEDGE OF GOD. When Jesus calls us to pray, he says that we do not need to use empty phrases and the repetition of many words to get God to hear us, "for your Father knows what you need before you ask him" (Matt. 6:8). This raises a common question: Why should we pray, if God already knows what we need? Jesus' statement sounds at first like a disincentive rather than a motivation to pray. But when we remember that prayer is a central part of a relationship with God as our Father, we can see how Jesus' words encourage prayer. A human father may know what a daughter wants before she asks, but he often waits for her to ask before he gladly gives it. In a similar way, God knows what we need before we pray, but he invites us to participate in the process of his blessing us. Prayer is an essential part of a true relationship with God.

Personal Implications

Reflect on how to apply what you have learned in this text to your everyday life. Make notes below on personal implications of (1) the *Gospel Glimpses*, (2) the

Whole-Bible Connections, (3) the *Theological Soundings*, and (4) this passage as a whole. Also write down what you have learned that can lead you to praise God, repent of sin, trust his gracious promises, and live in obedience to him.

1. Gospel Glimpses

2. Whole-Bible Connections

3. Theological Soundings

4. Matthew 6:1–8

As You Finish This Unit . . .

Take a moment to pray and ask for the Lord's blessing and help as you continue in this study of the Sermon on the Mount. And take a moment also to look back through this unit of study, to reflect on a few key things that the Lord may be teaching you—and perhaps to highlight and underline these things to review again in the future.

Definitions

[1] **Adoption** – The legal process by which a person gives the status of son or daughter to another person who is not his or her child by birth. The NT uses the term to describe the act by which God through the Spirit makes believers his children through the atoning death and resurrection of his one and only true Son, Jesus (see Romans 8; Galatians 4).

[2] **Idolatry** – In the Bible, idolatry usually refers to the worship of a physical object. Paul's comments in Colossians 3:5, however, suggest that idolatry can include covetousness, since it is essentially equivalent to worshiping material things.

Week 8: A Model for Prayer

Matthew 6:9–18

▲

Throughout much of the Sermon on the Mount Jesus calls his people to a "righteousness that exceeds," or is greater than, that of the scribes and Pharisees. This is a righteousness that is far removed from hypocritical religious acts and that instead flows from a transformed heart and is expressed in every part of life. Jesus calls his disciples to this righteousness (Matt. 5:17–20), illustrates it with six ethical examples (vv. 21–48), and then illustrates it further with three examples in the realm of religious devotion: giving, prayer, and fasting (6:1–18). In this section he expands his teaching on prayer to include what we refer to as the Lord's Prayer, and then he briefly addresses fasting. The Lord's Prayer is the heart of the Sermon on the Mount, both thematically and structurally. Jesus refers repeatedly to God as our Father in the Sermon on the Mount, and now he teaches us how to relate to our Father in prayer. This is a model for true communion with God.

The Big Picture

In contrast to hypocritical or empty praying, Jesus teaches his disciples how to pray and fast rightly.

Reflection and Discussion

Carefully and thoughtfully read this section of Jesus' teaching, Matthew 6:9–18. Then use the provided questions to help you think more deeply about the text. (See *ESV Study Bible* notes on pages 1831–1832; online at www.esv.org.)

What should come to our mind when we begin prayer by addressing God as "our Father in heaven" (Matt. 6:9)? How does this encourage us to pray (consider also 1 Pet. 5:7)?

The first topic in this prayer is not a declaration that God's name[1] *is* hallowed; it is a request that God's name *be* hallowed. Throughout the Old Testament, a name functions as a summary or shorthand for one's identity. And to be "hallowed" means to be holy, sanctified, or set apart. In light of this, restate or paraphrase this first request in your own words.

The kingdom of heaven is God's saving and renewing reign through Jesus. It is already present and spreading in the world as the church (Matt. 4:17, 23; 12:28), yet it will not come in its fullness until Jesus returns. What are a few examples of what we expect when we pray for God's kingdom to come (6:10)?

The Bible distinguishes between God's *sovereign* will,[2] which always happens and which mysteriously includes both the good and the evil actions of humanity, and God's *moral* will, which refers to his commands that people may or may not obey. Which aspect of God's will is in view in Matthew 6:10? What are a few areas of life in which you long to see God's will done?

While the first three requests of this prayer are more directly God-centered, the next three requests focus more on our personal needs, the first of which is the petition for "our daily bread" (v. 11). This prayer assumes that God providentially and kindly oversees the whole process that results in a meal's being placed in front of us. There are many people and processes that contribute to bringing even the simplest of meals from the field to the table. Write down several of the concrete and specific means God uses to bring you the food you eat, then thank him for each one.

Jesus often uses the language of "debts" (Matt. 6:12; see also Luke 7:41–48) to refer to that for which we need to be forgiven. In what way are sins appropriately called "debts"? How deep is our debt to the Lord (see Matt. 18:24)?

James 1:13–15 says that God cannot be tempted by evil, nor does he tempt anyone. What, then, does Jesus mean in Matthew 6:13?

In Matthew 6:14–15 Jesus connects our forgiveness from God with our willingness to forgive others. In other words, only the forgiving are forgiven. How do we understand the connection between the two—our forgiveness from God and our forgiveness toward others? Consider how Matthew 18:23–35 helps us understand the connection (see also Eph. 4:31–5:2; Col. 3:13).

The content of our prayers reveals our values. In light of this, what do the requests of the Lord's Prayer teach us to prioritize in life? What are some ways in which you can better cultivate these priorities?

Fasting is about forgoing food in order to express devotion to God. What similarities do you see between Matthew 6:16–18 and 6:1–8? What, then, is Jesus' main point?

Christians often fast in order to amplify prayer and to express a particular longing to the Lord. What are a few things that you long for God to do in your life or the lives of others? How can you plan to pray and fast for these in light of Jesus' teaching here?

Read through the following three sections on *Gospel Glimpses*, *Whole-Bible Connections*, and *Theological Soundings*. Then take time to consider the *Personal Implications* these sections have for you.

▶ Gospel Glimpses

PRAYING TO A FATHER OF LOVE. When Jesus teaches us to address God in prayer, he chooses one of God's titles in particular: "Our Father" (Matt. 6:9). Prayer does not mean coming to "our employer," reporting for duty. It does not mean coming to "the force," ready to experience a surge of energy. It is coming, very personally and very relationally, to our Father who loves us. Prayer is essentially relational. Prayer is speaking to the God who cares for us with fatherly affection. Since Jesus' own death, resurrection, and ascension secure our eternal adoption into God's family, we come humbly and boldly to the Father by grace (Eph. 1:5).

FORGIVENESS. Jesus tells his disciples to pray, "Forgive us our debts" (Matt. 6:12), but he does not yet say just how much it will cost him for this prayer to be answered. Forgiveness is gracious and free for the one who requests it, but it is costly for the one who extends it. Jesus is on his way to the cross, where he will pay *all* of our debts with his very life. As he will tell his disciples later, "The Son of Man came not to be served but to serve, and to give his life as a ransom[3] for many" (Matt. 20:28). The payment we owe to God for our debt of sin is eternal death, and this is what Jesus paid on the cross so that we would not have to do so. God has now "forgiven us all our trespasses, by canceling the record of debt that stood against us with its legal demands. This he set aside, nailing it to the cross" (Col. 2:13–14).

Whole-Bible Connections

SANCTIFYING GOD'S NAME. The prayer "Hallowed be your name" (Matt. 6:9) is not a praise but a plea. It is a request that God would cause his name to be sanctified, honored, and regarded as holy. It is a request that God's name would no longer be profaned but honored in the world. The background to this request is Ezekiel 36. God sent Israel into exile because they had "profaned my holy name" (Ezek. 36:20). But he added, "I had concern for my holy name," and he promised to act "not for your sake . . . but for the sake of my holy name" (vv. 21–22). God said, "I will vindicate the holiness of my great name, which has been profaned among the nations, and which you have profaned among them" (v. 23). This is connected to God's promise to bring a new covenant in which he would forgive sins, give new hearts, and send the Holy Spirit so that people no longer rejected him but honored and obeyed him (vv. 26–27). Jesus has come to bring these blessings through his death and resurrection. He calls us now to ask the Father to spread these blessings in the world so that God's name might be hallowed.

YOUR KINGDOM COME. When Jesus teaches us to pray "Your kingdom come" (Matt. 6:10), he is teaching us to ask God to spread his rule and reign in the world. The promise of God's kingdom was an especially prominent part of the message of the prophet Isaiah. The "good news" (lit., "gospel") that Isaiah announced is summarized with two key clauses: "Behold your God" (Isa. 40:9) and "Your God reigns" (52:7). Both of these phrases announce the good news that God will return to his people as a king, he will reign, and he will rescue them from their enemies, including the powerful enemies of sin and death. These promises began to be fulfilled with the coming of Christ. Jesus is God in the flesh, truly God and truly man, who came to rescue his people and reign over all things. God's kingdom comes as the church spreads the gospel and more people submit to Jesus' gracious reign, and it will come finally and fully upon his return.

Theological Soundings

A FRAMEWORK FOR PRAYER. Prayer is clearly important, but *how* should we pray? The Lord's Prayer is not intended merely to be recited; it functions as a framework for prayer. It teaches us about the God to whom we pray ("Our Father in heaven") and then provides two categories of prayer, each of which contains three requests. The first category is primarily Godward, focusing on (1) God's reputation's being honored, (2) his kingdom's spreading, and (3) his will's being done. The second category is primarily focused on our needs: (1) our daily sustenance, (2) forgiveness of sins, and (3) deliverance from evil. When we pray, we can use each of these requests as a summary heading and then pray various requests under each one. This is how we let the six priorities of the Lord's Prayer shape our requests.

TEMPTATION AND THE SOVEREIGNTY OF GOD. Jesus invites us to pray "Lead us not into temptation, but deliver us from evil" (Matt. 6:13). The Bible teaches God's sovereignty over all things while also upholding his good character and good purposes in all he does, yet leaving quite a bit of mystery about how this all works. God's sovereignty over temptation is an example of this. James is clear that God does not tempt anyone with evil but that "Each person is tempted when he is lured and enticed by his own desire" (James 1:14). Nevertheless, the Bible also affirms that nothing happens apart from God's will and that he will not allow us to be tempted beyond our ability to withstand (Eph. 1:11; 1 Cor. 10:13).

Personal Implications

Reflect on how to apply what you have learned in this text to your everyday life. Make notes below on personal implications of (1) the *Gospel Glimpses*, (2) the *Whole-Bible Connections*, (3) the *Theological Soundings*, and (4) this passage as a whole. Also write down what you have learned that can lead you to praise God, repent of sin, trust his gracious promises, and live in obedience to him.

1. Gospel Glimpses

2. Whole-Bible Connections

3. Theological Soundings

4. Matthew 6:9–18

_____

_____

_____

_____

_____

_____

_____

As You Finish This Unit . . .

Take a moment to pray and ask for the Lord's blessing and help as you continue in this study of Matthew 6:9–18. And take a moment also to look back through this unit of study, to reflect on a few key things that the Lord may be teaching you—and perhaps to highlight and underline these things to review again in the future.

Definitions

[1] **Name** – In the Psalms, the name of the Lord is often the object of religious affections—such as praise, love, trust, and hope (e.g., Pss. 5:11; 7:17; 8:1, 9; 18:49; 33:21; 92:1; 96:2; 102:15). Deuteronomy 12:5, 11 speaks of God's "name" dwelling in the sanctuary; i.e., the Lord's name is a way of speaking about his personal presence (see Lev. 19:12; Deut. 6:13) or the sum of his revealed character (Ex. 34:6).

[2] **Sovereignty** – Supreme and independent power and authority. Sovereignty over all things is a distinctive attribute of God (1 Tim. 6:15–16). He directs all things to carry out his purposes (Rom. 8:28–29).

[3] **Ransom** – A price paid to redeem, or buy back, someone who had become enslaved or something that had been lost to someone else. Jesus described his ministry as serving others and giving his life as a ransom for many (Matt. 20:28).

Week 9: Replacing Greed and Anxiety with Generosity and Faith

Matthew 6:19–34

▲

The Place of the Passage

After pronouncing the Beatitudes and issuing the call to live out the light of the gospel of the kingdom (Matt. 5:1–16), Jesus announced his Scripture-fulfilling call to a wholehearted and whole-life righteousness (5:17–20), which he then illustrated with ethical (5:21–48) and devotional examples (6:1–18). In the previous section we heard Jesus' call to give, pray, and fast for the reward from God rather than the praise of people. Jesus now continues in a similar vein by calling us to store up treasures in heaven rather than on earth (vv. 19–21). The common theme throughout this section is wealth: storing up treasures in heaven (vv. 19–21), living with generosity (vv. 22–23), serving God rather than money (v. 24), and learning to trust God and seek his kingdom rather than the things of life (vv. 25–34). In all this Jesus shows us how to relate to money as we pursue the true life of flourishing in his kingdom.

The Big Picture

Jesus calls us to resist greediness, stinginess, and anxiety about wealth and instead to serve God and trust in his provision.

Reflection and Discussion

Carefully and thoughtfully read this section of Jesus' teaching, Matthew 6:19–34. Then use the provided questions to help you think more deeply about the text. (See *ESV Study Bible* notes on pages 1832–1833; online at www.esv.org.)

Laying Up Treasures in Heaven (Matt. 6:19–21)

Jesus masterfully transitions from one topic to the next in the Sermon on the Mount. Very often what he says at these transitional moments wraps up the previous topic while also introducing the next one. What common words and themes do you see in Matthew 6:19–21 that relate to what came before, in verses 1–18? What words and themes relate to what comes next, in verses 22–34?

What does Jesus mean by "treasures in heaven," and why is storing them up wiser than storing up treasures on earth (Matt. 6:20)? What are a few practical ways to store up treasure in heaven?

Jesus recognizes that "Where your treasure is, there your heart will be also" (Matt. 6:21). When have you seen your own heart become too wrapped up in something you invested in or purchased? What is Jesus saying to do instead?

Generosity and Worship (Matt. 6:22–24)

Jesus says our eyes are like lamps for our body, and whether our eyes are "good" or "bad" will determine whether the rest of our body becomes full of light or of darkness (Matt. 6:21–23). This Hebrew idiom is seen in wisdom literature such as Proverbs, in which someone with a "good" or a "healthy eye" is generous, whereas someone with a "bad eye" is stingy (see Prov. 22:9, where the Hebrew for "good eye" is translated "bountiful eye"; and 23:6, where "bad eye" is translated "stingy"). Note also the surrounding context in Matthew 6 and how Jesus focuses on our heart's orientation toward wealth (Matt. 6:19–20, 24). How would you summarize Jesus' point in verses 22–24 in light of these facts?

How can money function as a master that we serve and worship? How is it true that serving money and serving God are incompatible?

Anxiety and Trust (Matt. 6:25–34)

Anxiety is a complex topic, addressed in numerous ways throughout the Bible. Here Jesus addresses our tendency to be anxious about a few particular matters (Matt. 6:25, 31). What are they? What matters have you been anxious about recently?

Jesus does not merely command people not to be anxious about their needs; he gently reasons with us, appealing to how the Father values us and cares for us. What are the specific reasons for and examples of God's love for us that Jesus gives in Matthew 6:25–34 to help us not to be anxious? Which one is most significant to you?

Jesus calls the disciples "you of little faith" (Matt. 6:30). What does this indicate about the nature of faith? What does it also teach us about the nature of anxiety?

Summarize what you have already learned in the Sermon on the Mount about the two topics Jesus mentions in Matthew 6:33: God's kingdom and God's righteousness.

What does Matthew 6:25–34 teach us about God? How do these truths and this vision of God help us to trust him?

What similarities do you see between Matthew 6:25–34 and 1 Peter 5:6–7? What are a few matters you want to bring to the Lord in prayer in light of these encouragements?

Read through the following three sections on *Gospel Glimpses*, *Whole-Bible Connections*, and *Theological Soundings*. Then take time to consider the *Personal Implications* these sections have for you.

Gospel Glimpses

SERVING A BETTER MASTER. Jesus says plainly, "You cannot serve God and money" (Matt. 6:24). It is not that we are able to serve both but should not—his point is that we cannot do so even if we tried. God and money are incompatible. Whatever we trust as our highest good, whatever we trust as our source of provision and security, that will be the god we serve. We will look either to the fleeting and unstable master of money to provide everything we need or to the Father who owns everything and loves us through Christ as his dear children. More than that, when we come to Christ in faith, not only do we have God as our Father, but he promises to give us all things in Christ (6:32–33; see 1 Cor. 3:21–23). In light of this, it is clear that we cannot serve God and money—and why would we even want to try?

YOU ARE VALUABLE. Jesus wants us to know how valuable we are to the Father. As we fret about the necessities of life, Jesus calls us to watch how God the Father takes care of the birds. He feeds them because he values them. And Jesus asks, "Are you not of more value than they?" (Matt. 6:26). Of course we are! God made and cares for his creation, but humanity is the pinnacle of his creation, uniquely made in his image, set over the birds and all the animals (Gen. 1:26–27). It is true that our sin is appalling and that we deserve eternal death for it, yet God still loves us. He says of sinful Israel in Isaiah 43:4, "You are precious in my eyes, and honored, and I love you." And he has proven this by giving his own Son for us on the cross. As the Puritan pastor Thomas Goodwin put it, God values us above the world, "and he gave real testimony of this in giving his Son, which was more than a thousand worlds." Surely we can trust this kind of God, with this kind of love, to care for us.

Whole-Bible Connections

TREASURE IN HEAVEN. Jesus calls us to lay up for ourselves treasures not on earth but in heaven (Matt. 6:19–20). Jesus invites us to set our eyes not merely above, in heaven, but on our eternal future. When we lay up treasures in heaven, we acknowledge that we are willing to wait. And for what are we waiting? We are waiting for the coming of Christ and the glory of the new creation.[1] The apostle Paul writes similarly, "Set your minds on things that are above, not on things that are on earth. For you have died, and your life is hidden with Christ in God. When Christ who is your life appears, then you also will appear with him in glory" (Col. 3:2–4).

SERVICE IN IDOLATRY. Jesus calls us to forsake money as our master and to serve God alone (Matt. 6:24). The need to forsake idols such as money began as soon as sin entered the world. God created humanity to serve and worship him, but man has served and worshiped the creation instead of the Creator (Gen. 2:15; Rom. 1:21–22). When God rescued Israel through the exodus,[2] he called them to reject idolatry and to worship him alone (Ex. 20:2–6, 17). And when Jesus came and brought the kingdom of God into the world, he invited all to serve God alone rather than money or what it can buy. All who trust in Jesus will battle with the heart-lure of the false gods of money, comfort, pleasure, and so forth, but we look ahead to the new creation, where our hearts will be happily and eternally set on the triune God as our good master (Rev. 21:3).

Theological Soundings

GROWING IN FAITH. When Jesus calls his disciples to trust the Father rather than to be anxious for necessities, he calls them "you of little faith" (Matt. 6:30). Jesus often draws attention to their "little faith" (8:26; 14:31; 16:8; 17:20). These are not unbelievers; they are disciples of Jesus who do trust the Father. Yet at times their trust is not much but little, not strong but weak. This shows us that, while our conversion[3] is the decisive moment at which we move from unbelief to belief, it is also true that the Christian life involves growing from little belief to more belief. Once we enter into the realm of trusting Christ, this trust grows in degrees. It rises and falls in various circumstances. We may often feel like the man who cried out, "I believe; help my unbelief!" (Mark 9:24). This is why the Christian life is a life of learning to trust Christ more truly and deeply in every area of life.

GOD'S PROVIDENCE. Jesus teaches that God the Father feeds the birds of the air, beautifies the grass of the field, and provides our necessities for life (Matt. 6:25–33). This assumes the doctrine of God's providence, which refers to God's thorough and wise care for his creation. The Westminster Catechism summarizes the biblical doctrine of God's providence in this way: "God's works of providence are his most holy, wise, and powerful preserving and governing all his creatures, and all their actions." God governs all things and cares for his creation according to his wisdom and for his glory.

Personal Implications

Reflect on how to apply what you have learned in this text to your everyday life. Make notes below on personal implications of (1) the *Gospel Glimpses*, (2) the *Whole-Bible Connections*, (3) the *Theological Soundings*, and (4) this passage as a whole. Also write down what you have learned that can lead you to praise God, repent of sin, trust his gracious promises, and live in obedience to him.

1. Gospel Glimpses

2. Whole-Bible Connections

3. Theological Soundings

----

4. Matthew 6:19–34

> ## As You Finish This Unit . . .

Take a moment to pray and ask for the Lord's blessing and help as you continue in this study of Matthew 6:19–34. And take a moment also to look back through this unit of study, to reflect on a few key things that the Lord may be teaching you—and perhaps to highlight and underline these things to review again in the future.

Definitions

[1] **New creation** – The world to come (Heb. 2:5) that stands in contrast with this "present evil age" (see Gal. 1:4; 6:15). From the moment humanity alienated itself from God, this present world in all its facets has been corrupted by sin. Christ's resurrection marks the dawn of a new world, a new creation, in which everything is as it was created to be. Through union with Christ by the Spirit, believers are a first part of this new creation (2 Cor. 5:17), and, when Christ returns to judge and complete his redeeming work, the entire world will experience its transformation into this new creation.

[2] **The exodus** – The departure of the people of Israel from Egypt and their journey to Mount Sinai under Moses' leadership (Exodus 1–19; Numbers 33). The exodus demonstrated God's power and providence for his people, who had been enslaved by the Egyptians. The annual festival of Passover commemorates God's final plague upon the Egyptians, resulting in Israel's release from Egypt.

[3] **Conversion** – The result of turning away from sin, accepting the truth of the gospel of Jesus Christ, and submitting to him. Conversion is the human activity mirroring the divine activity of regeneration (granting of new birth).

WEEK 10: A NEW VISION FOR RELATIONSHIPS

Matthew 7:1–12

The Place of the Passage

Jesus brings the central section of the Sermon the Mount to a conclusion. After the introductory Beatitudes and the call to live out the light of the gospel of the kingdom in the world (Matt. 5:1–16), Jesus announced that he came to fulfill the Law and the Prophets and that he was bringing about a greater righteousness for his people (5:17–20). After unfolding this vision with several ethical examples (5:21–48), devotional practices (6:1–18), and instruction addressing our relationship with anxiety and money (6:19–34), Jesus applies this to our personal relationships as well (7:1–12). He first corrects a hypocritical tone of judgmentalism (7:1–6) and then confronts our need for expectancy in prayer (vv. 7–11). He concludes not only this section but the whole central section of the Sermon on the Mount with a vision for how we are to treat others. This section thus unfolds his vision for our relationships with one another and with our heavenly Father.

The Big Picture

Jesus offers a new vision for relationships by correcting hypocritical judgmentalism, encouraging expectant prayer, and calling us to treat others as we wish they would treat us.

Reflection and Discussion

Carefully and thoughtfully read this section of Jesus' teaching, Matthew 7:1–12. Then use the provided questions to help you think more deeply about the text. (See *ESV Study Bible* notes on pages 1833–1834; online at www.esv.org.)

Relationships in the Church and the World (Matt. 7:1–6)

Jesus' command to "judge not, that you be not judged" (Matt. 7:1) is well known but often misunderstood. Many people understand this to mean, "Do not say that someone's doctrine or behavior is wrong." But what do you see in the context of Matthew 7:1–5 that indicates that this is not what Jesus means? (Consider also vv. 6, 15–20.)

In your own words, summarize the meaning of Jesus' illustration of the speck and the log in Matthew 7:3–4. Why is this teaching important?

Jesus calls those who are pridefully judgmental toward others "hypocritical." In what way are they being hypocritical? How is this similar to the issues Jesus addressed in Matthew 6:1–18?

In a sentence, summarize the main point of Matthew 7:1–5.

Jesus is speaking to an important issue in relationships within the Christian community. What are some features of a community marked by hypocritical and prideful attitudes of judgmentalism? In contrast to this, what are features of the type of community Jesus is creating with his teaching in Matthew 7:1–5?

In the first century, people often despised dogs and pigs and valued holy things and pearls. Although some dispute what Jesus means, if that which is valuable refers to the Christian message, and if the animals refer to those who spurn the message, then what is Jesus' point? How would Matthew 10:14 support this understanding?

Relationship with God (Matt. 7:7–11)

What is Jesus' main point in Matthew 7:7–8? Why do you think Jesus piles up similar and repeated concepts and words here?

We often ignore God and refuse to pray because of our sneaking suspicion that he is aloof or stingy. But what does Matthew 7:9–11 teach us about the character of God? How should this encourage us to pray?

Summary: Do to Others What You Wish They Would Do to You (Matt. 7:12)

When Jesus says that his commandment ("Whatever you wish that others would do to you, do also to them") "*is* the Law and the Prophets" (Matt. 7:12), what does he mean? Consider Matthew 22:40, Romans 13:8, and Galatians 5:14.

Think about the Golden Rule in the context of the Sermon on the Mount. Notice the similarity between Matthew 7:12 and Jesus' introductory statement of

Matthew 5:17. What are a few examples of how this serves to summarize what Jesus has taught in the portion of the sermon found between these two verses?

What would look different in your next few days if this vision of selfless love captured your imagination and God's Spirit enabled you to live it out? Be specific.

Read through the following three sections on *Gospel Glimpses, Whole-Bible Connections*, and *Theological Soundings*. Then take time to consider the *Personal Implications* these sections have for you.

▶ Gospel Glimpses

A NEW KIND OF CULTURE. The Sermon on the Mount is not a legalistic checklist to accomplish. It is a gracious invitation to join a new way of being human. This sermon is Jesus' vision for the culture of love he is creating through his death, resurrection, and outpoured Spirit. He *models* it before us in his exemplary life, he *teaches* it to us in the Sermon on the Mount, and he *creates* it in us by his outpoured Spirit. This is a counterculture of grace, love, and kindness. Left to ourselves, we create communities of hypocritical judgmentalism, we ignore God because we think he is stingy, and we expect others to treat us better than we treat them. But Jesus came to free us from sin and to create a culture in which we look at the log in our own eye before helping others with the speck in theirs (Matt. 7:1–5). Jesus came to create a culture in which we look expectantly to our generous Father to meet our needs (vv. 7–11). He came to create a culture in which we do to others whatever we wish they would do to us (v. 12). And he welcomes anyone and everyone to be a part of this culture.

THE GIVER OF GOOD. When Jesus encourages us to pray, he does not merely say, "Pray because you should pray." No, he unfolds before us the generous heart of the Father. He encourages us to think about the best fathers we know, the ones who only and always give good gifts to their children, and then he teaches us that our Father in heaven is even more generous than that (Matt. 7:9–11). God is more generous than the most generous person you have ever met. He is the giver of all good. He gives good gifts—even the Holy Spirit (Luke 11:13)—to those who ask him. There could be no better encouragement to pray.

Whole-Bible Connections

THE OLD TESTAMENT AND THE GOLDEN RULE. Jesus provides a beautiful summary of his teaching with what we now call the Golden Rule: "Whatever you wish that others would do to you, do also to them" (Matt. 7:12). He goes on to point out that this rule is the summary not simply of his own teaching but of the Old Testament also, as he adds, "this is the Law and the Prophets." Earlier in the Sermon on the Mount Jesus said he came not to abolish the law and the prophets but to fulfill them (5:17). The Golden Rule is one way in which Jesus demonstrates that his message does not contradict the Old Testament but fulfills it. Jesus has come to create a kingdom filled with forgiven and transformed sinners who not merely agree with the Golden Rule but begin to embody it.

Theological Soundings

HUMAN SINFULNESS. When Jesus teaches us to pray, he commends the generosity of fathers, affirming that they would not give a stone to a child who asked for bread, nor a serpent when asked for a fish (Matt. 7:9–10). Yet then he says, "If you then, who are evil, know how to give good gifts . . ." (v. 11). In Jesus' view, human fathers are a model of generosity and care, but they are also, in his words, "evil." This is true of even the best people—loving and generous fathers—according to Jesus. We are not as bad as we could be, but something is so deeply wrong that Jesus can summarize us with this singularly damning word. The Bible teaches that we are not merely sinners because we sin; fundamentally, we sin because we are sinners. Ever since the fall,[1] when Adam sinned, every person has been born with a sinful nature, and so we are "by nature children of wrath" (Eph. 2:3) and thus in need not only of forgiveness but of regeneration.[2]

THE ETHIC OF LOVE. Ethics is the study of morality, justice, and virtue. Jesus addresses various ethical topics throughout his ministry. In the Sermon on the

Mount Jesus summarizes the whole of our ethical responsibility toward others with the Golden Rule: "Whatever you wish that others would do to you, do also to them" (Matt. 7:12). Elsewhere he summarizes this responsibility toward others by stating, "You shall love your neighbor as yourself" (22:39). In each case he notes how his teaching summarizes the ethical teaching of our responsibility toward others in the Old Testament (7:12; 22:40). These two statements complement one another, showing that at the heart of Christian ethics is to love others and treat them as we wish they would treat us.

Personal Implications

Reflect on how to apply what you have learned in this text to your everyday life. Make notes below on personal implications of (1) the *Gospel Glimpses*, (2) the *Whole-Bible Connections*, (3) the *Theological Soundings*, and (4) this passage as a whole. Also write down what you have learned that can lead you to praise God, repent of sin, trust his gracious promises, and live in obedience to him.

1. Gospel Glimpses

2. Whole-Bible Connections

3. Theological Soundings

4. Matthew 7:1–12

`.`---

> ## As You Finish This Unit . . .

Take a moment to pray and ask for the Lord's blessing and help as you continue in this study of Matthew 7:1–12. And take a moment also to look back through this unit of study, to reflect on a few key things that the Lord may be teaching you—and perhaps to highlight and underline these things to review again in the future.

Definitions

[1] **The fall** – Adam and Eve's disobedience of God by eating the fruit of the tree of the knowledge of good and evil, resulting in their loss of innocence and favor with God and the introduction of sin and its effects into the world.

[2] **Regeneration** – The Holy Spirit's work of bringing spiritual life to a person, thus enabling him or her to trust, love, and follow God. Essentially equivalent to what is often referred to as being "born again" (John 3:7) or "saved" (5:34).

WEEK 11: TWO WAYS AND TWO TREES

Matthew 7:13–20

▲

The Place of the Passage

Throughout the Sermon on the Mount Jesus has set before his disciples the good life of blessedness and flourishing. The Beatitudes introduced this vision, and then Jesus unfolded this further by contrasting the life of true righteousness with a hypocritical and self-oriented life. Now Jesus begins to bring his sermon to a close with a series of contrasts, leading those who hear to a point of decision regarding him and his claims. He contrasts two gates and two ways to illustrate the decision all must make, and then he exposes false teachers by contrasting two kinds of trees. In all of this, he leads his hearers to understand the truth and goodness of the way of his kingdom and to embrace it wholeheartedly.

The Big Picture

Jesus teaches the importance of aligning decisively to his way and his teaching by means of illustrations of two ways and two kinds of trees.

Reflection and Discussion

Carefully and thoughtfully read this section of Jesus' teaching, Matthew 7:13–20. Then use the provided questions to help you think more deeply about the text. (See *ESV Study Bible* notes on page 1834; online at www.esv.org.)

The Narrow Way versus the Wide Way (Matt. 7:13–14)

Jesus begins to bring his teaching to a conclusion by contrasting two gates and two ways. What is the "gate" that Jesus calls people to enter and the "way" he calls people to join?

Many people think there are multiple ways to salvation and eternal life[1] and that most, or even all, people will be saved in the end. How would you respond to such claims in light of Jesus' illustration here?

What does each of the following texts teach us about the exclusivity of Jesus— that is, that there is only one "gate" and one "way" of salvation, and that this way is through Jesus Christ? Consider also John 14:6; Acts 4:12; 1 Timothy 2:5; and 1 John 5:11–12.

Jesus says the gate is "narrow" and the way is "hard" that leads to life (Matt. 7:13–14). Sometimes Jesus highlights the easiness of salvation: we simply trust him, come to him for rest, and receive life in his name (Matt. 11:28; John 1:12–13; 3:16). At other times he highlights how difficult it is truly to receive his grace, trust him, and follow him (Matt. 19:23–24; Luke 9:62; 14:26–30). How do these perspectives fit together?

What aspects of Jesus' teaching in the Sermon on the Mount seem uniquely hard for you to embrace or practice?

The Healthy versus the Diseased Tree (Matt. 7:15–20)

What does it mean for a false prophet to come in sheep's clothing (Matt. 7:15)? What are some modern examples of the way in which false prophets disguise themselves in order to appear winsome, trustworthy, or appealing?

What do we learn about false teachers and false teaching from each of these texts: 1 Timothy 1:3–7; 4:1–5; 2 Timothy 3:1–9; and Titus 1:10–16?

What are a few common messages that false prophets and false teachers promote today? Why are these messages so appealing to people? How do you resist their lure?

Since false prophets look like faithful disciples on the outside, we often cannot discern their true motives or character from their outward appearance. What does Jesus mean when he issues the criterion of recognizing them by their fruits (Matt. 7:16)? In light of this, what are a few ways in which you can spot a false prophet today?

In your own words, summarize the point of Jesus' teaching in Matthew 7:17–20. How does this relate to what Jesus has just said in verses 15–16?

What are three ways in which Christians can fortify themselves against the deception of false teaching?

Read through the following three sections on *Gospel Glimpses, Whole-Bible Connections*, and *Theological Soundings*. Then take time to consider the *Personal Implications* these sections have for you.

Gospel Glimpses

THE NARROW GATE OF GRACE. Trusting Jesus is the easiest thing in the world to do, and yet it requires that we humble ourselves and admit that we need his salvation, which is hard for prideful people to do. It also requires that we believe that he really is this gracious—that he would welcome "repeat offenders" of his glory with such open arms. This is hard to believe because it is so radically and counterintuitively *kind*. Receiving grace with empty hands of faith is easy, but it requires that we let go of our prideful commitment to the claims that we are not all that bad and that we can do something to earn God's favor. Amazingly, it is the very posture of humble faith that produces a transformed life of obedience and leads us to embrace hardship in Christ's name.

ONE WAY OF SALVATION. Jesus describes a narrow gate that leads to life and a wide gate that leads to destruction (Matt. 7:13–14). He says elsewhere that he is the only way to the Father (John 14:6). Some may hear this and think it sounds like bad news, wondering why Jesus sounds so exclusive. However, Jesus is the only way to the Father because there is no other possible way for our sin to be forgiven besides the cross of Christ. We cannot live a good enough life to cancel the eternal debt required for our sins. No other philosophy or religion acknowledges the depth of evil in the human heart, and no other philosophy or religion shows the greatness of love in the heart of God. The exclusivity of Jesus as the only way of salvation points us to the greatness and graciousness of our salvation. He is the only solution to our deepest problem.

Whole-Bible Connections

THE PROMISE OF LIFE. As Jesus calls people to enter the narrow gate and follow the hard way, he promises that such a response leads to "life" (Matt. 7:14). This promise of "life" is not only everlasting existence but true joy, flourishing, and enjoyment of God's presence in a new creation forever. It is the flourishing for which we were made, the heart of which is knowing God (John 17:3). We were originally created for this fullness of life in Eden (Genesis 1–2), but humanity rejected God and earned an eternal future of death (Genesis 3). Jesus came to take our death on himself on the cross, he rose again as the first one to experience the resurrection life, and he now extends forgiveness and a share in life with him forever.

Theological Soundings

REGENERATION. Jesus repeatedly indicates that real Christians will live transformed lives. He teaches us to identify true or false teachers by their fruits, for healthy trees bear good fruit while diseased trees bear bad fruit (Matt. 7:15–20). He also teaches that those who confess him as Lord but do not live transformed lives will not, in fact, be saved (vv. 21–23). This assumes the doctrine of regeneration—that those who are truly saved are "born again," "regenerated," given new and transformed hearts to live transformed lives (John 3:3–8; 1 Cor. 5:17; Eph. 2:4–5; 1 John 2:29). In other words, all those who experience justification[2] will also experience sanctification.[3] Those who come to Christ do not merely make a mental assent to truth; they are given new hearts with new desires and thus they live transformed lives.

SOUND DOCTRINE. Theological faithfulness matters. Jesus warned his people to "beware of false prophets" (Matt. 7:15) because false doctrine is dangerous. False teachers misrepresent the truth. They seek to bend reality to the will of the teacher rather than submitting their lives to the will of their Maker. False doctrine also often leads to immorality, for that which people believe inevitably shapes how they live. Followers of Jesus embrace the importance of both gospel doctrine and gospel character. Every church must embrace the necessity of upholding both truth and love and must therefore reject false teaching and immoral living.

Personal Implications

Reflect on how to apply what you have learned in this text to your everyday life. Make notes below on personal implications of (1) the *Gospel Glimpses*, (2) the *Whole-Bible Connections*, (3) the *Theological Soundings*, and (4) this passage as a whole. Also write down what you have learned that can lead you to praise God, repent of sin, trust his gracious promises, and live in obedience to him.

1. Gospel Glimpses

2. Whole-Bible Connections

3. Theological Soundings

4. Matthew 7:13–20

> ## As You Finish This Unit . . .

Take a moment to pray and ask for the Lord's blessing and help as you continue in this study of Matthew 7:13–20. And take a moment also to look back through this unit of study, to reflect on a few key things that the Lord may be teaching you—and perhaps to highlight and underline these things to review again in the future.

Definitions

[1] **Eternal life** – For believers, the new life that begins with trust in Jesus Christ alone for salvation and continues after physical death with an eternity in God's presence, with resurrected and glorified bodies in the new heavens and the new earth.

[2] **Justification** – The moment God declares a Christ-trusting sinner to be in right standing before him; i.e., becoming positionally righteous.

[3] **Sanctification** – The incremental, Spirit-empowered process of being conformed to Christ's image; i.e., becoming progressively more righteous.

93

WEEK 12: A CALL TO DECISIVENESS

TWO DESTINIES AND TWO FOUNDATIONS

Matthew 7:21–29

Jesus began to bring the Sermon on the Mount to a conclusion in Matthew 7:13. From that point on he introduced a series of contrasts that led us to a point of decisiveness about him. He emphasized how there are only two ways to life, a narrow way and a broad way, and we must choose the one we will follow (vv. 13–14). There are also two kinds of trees: healthy trees that bear the fruit of good works and diseased trees that do not (vv. 15–20). Now Jesus introduces two kinds of people who claim that Jesus is Lord:[1] those who claim his lordship without submitting to it and those who gladly do the will of God. There are also two kinds of builders: those who build their house on the foundation of Christ's teaching and those who do not. By the end of the sermon the astonished crowds—and all who hear him—must decide on which side of these contrasts they are.

The Big Picture

Jesus uses several contrasts to illustrate the point that there are ultimately only two ways to respond to his message.

Reflection and Discussion

Carefully and thoughtfully read this final section of Jesus' teaching in the Sermon on the Mount, Matthew 7:21–29. Then use the provided questions to help you think more deeply about the text. (See *ESV Study Bible* notes on pages 1834–1835; online at www.esv.org.)

A Warning: Beware of Self-Deception and False-Assurance (Matt. 7:21–23)

In Matthew 7:21–23 Jesus identifies several characteristics that do not necessarily indicate that someone is a true Christian. What are they? What other similar behaviors do professing Christians pursue that demonstrate that they are not necessarily true Christians (consider 1 Cor. 13:1–3)?

While Jesus identifies a number of characteristics that people may replicate without actually being a part of his kingdom, what are the key realities in Matthew 7:21–23 that confirm that someone is an authentic Christian?

At the heart of real Christianity is being known by Jesus (Matt. 7:23). Why is this essential (consider John 17:3 and Phil. 3:8–9)?

Write a sentence that summarizes in your own words Jesus' main point in Matthew 7:21–23.

A Call to Wisdom: Building on the Right Foundation (Matt. 7:24–27)

Jesus gives an illustration of two builders: two different people who build two different houses on two different foundations. What is the point that Jesus illustrates with this?

Jesus says that the wise will not only hear his words but also do them (Matt. 7:24). Read James 1:22–27 and 2:14–16. How does James make a similar point?

Although Jesus may have in mind various trials in life that expose our wisdom or folly, consider the context. Jesus is giving a series of contrasts: two pathways

(Matt. 7:13–14), two trees (vv. 15–20), two claims (vv. 21–23), and two builders (vv. 24–27). Review each of these and consider: what is the negative destination in each of these illustrations? To what, then, do you think the fall of the foolish builder's house refers?

Jesus brings his teaching to a conclusion in Matthew 7:24–27. How does this conclusion reinforce particular things he has taught throughout the sermon?

A Fitting Response: Astonishment at Jesus' Authority (Matt. 7:28–29)

Although Jesus initially directed his teaching at his disciples (Matt. 5:1), by the time he finishes we learn that crowds have been listening (7:28). They are astonished at what they have heard. Think back over the whole Sermon on the Mount. What aspects of Jesus' teaching have you found astonishing or surprising?

The crowds are particularly astonished at the uniqueness of Jesus' authority that comes through in his teaching. Look back over the whole Sermon on the Mount. What do you see that points to his unique authority?

As you reflect on your study of the Sermon on the Mount, what are three aspects of Jesus' teaching that have been most instructive, challenging, or encouraging to you?

What is the most important practical step you need to take in light of reading and studying Jesus' Sermon on the Mount?

Read through the following three sections on *Gospel Glimpses*, *Whole-Bible Connections*, and *Theological Soundings*. Then take time to consider the *Personal Implications* these sections have for you.

Gospel Glimpses

BEING KNOWN BY JESUS. Jesus says that many may call him "Lord" and even do quite amazing works in his name, but he will declare to many of them in the judgment,[2] "I never knew you" (Matt. 7:23). This shows that the nonnegotiable, essential, core reality of being a Christian is personal: knowing Jesus and being known by him. This is rightly alarming for any who are interested only in the miracles, reputation, or secondary benefits that come from being a Christian but do not know or love Christ himself. However, for all who come to Jesus for Jesus himself, for all who find Jesus himself to be the greatest treasure, this is not alarming; a relationship with Christ is the greatest part of what it means to be a Christian. At the heart of real Christianity is knowing—and, even better—being known by the triune God (1 Cor. 8:3; Gal. 4:8–9; Phil. 3:8–9). Eternal life itself is not just living forever; it is *knowing Jesus* now and forever (John 17:3).

A KIND SAVIOR, WISE SAGE, AND AUTHORITATIVE KING. Jesus calls everyone to be like a wise builder who builds his or her house on the firm foundation of Jesus' teaching (Matt. 7:24–27). We cannot take only part of Jesus' teaching as our foundation; we must take it whole. This means that Jesus is not just our Savior who forgives us but also our Sage who instructs us and our King who commands us. This is, in fact, wondrous news. Jesus does not forgive us and then leave us to fumble through life without wisdom. Neither is he a king who commands us with authority but will not forgive us when we fail. Instead, he is the perfect combination of grace, wisdom, and authority. He went to the cross to save us and now invites us to build our lives on his wise guidance.

Whole-Bible Connections

HEARING AND DOING. Jesus calls us not only to hear but also to do. He calls us to be a man or woman "who hears these words of mine and does them" (Matt. 7:24). Jesus is drawing on a long tradition, rooted in God's central commands to Israel in Deuteronomy. Moses said to Israel, "Now this is the commandment—the statutes and the rules—that the LORD your God commanded me to teach you, that you may do them" (Deut. 6:1). And, "Hear therefore, O Israel, and be careful to do them, that it may go well with you" (v. 3). Just as Israel was not only to hear but also to do, so too all who follow Jesus are called not only to hear but also to practice his teaching. James reinforces Jesus' message in his own way: "Be doers of the word, and not hearers only, deceiving yourselves" (James 1:22).

WISDOM AND FOLLY. Jesus concludes the Sermon on the Mount by urging listeners to be like a "wise man who built his house on the rock" rather than like a "foolish man who built his house on the sand" (Matt. 7:24–26). Jesus thus frames his entire teaching as wisdom. This draws on the theme of wisdom from the Old Testament. The book of Proverbs is the most obvious of this genre (Prov. 1:1–7), but many other Old Testament texts at critical points also call God's people to wisdom (Ps. 107:43; Dan. 12:3, 10; Hos. 14:9). Wisdom is about living well in God's world. The epitome of wisdom is trusting and following Jesus, while the height of folly is rejecting him while assuming life and eternity will still work out well for you.

Theological Soundings

ASSURANCE OF SALVATION. Jesus calls into question the ultimate salvation of those who claim him as Lord but do not do the will of his Father (Matt. 7:21). These kinds of statements lead some of us to wonder if we are saved. This question about the assurance of salvation is important, and the book of 1 John was written to help true believers answer it (1 John 5:13). Assurance of salvation is grounded ultimately in the work of Christ—his death and resurrection for our sins—and it is personally confirmed by the testimony of the Holy Spirit. However, assurance is confirmed in our lives also through three marks, or evidences, of authentic Christianity: belief, love, and obedience (1 John 5:1–2). True followers of Christ believe rightly about him (doctrinal evidence), love God and his people (relational evidence), and grow in obedience to God's commands (action evidence). These three strands form the triple cord of assurance.

Personal Implications

Reflect on how to apply what you have learned in this text to your everyday life. Make notes below on personal implications of (1) the *Gospel Glimpses*, (2) the *Whole-Bible Connections*, (3) the *Theological Soundings*, and (4) this passage as a whole. Also write down what you have learned that can lead you to praise God, repent of sin, trust his gracious promises, and live in obedience to him.

1. Gospel Glimpses

2. Whole-Bible Connections

3. Theological Soundings

4. Matthew 7:21–29

▶ As You Finish Studying the Sermon on the Mount . . .

We rejoice with you as you complete this study of the Sermon on the Mount! May what you have learned go with you day by day throughout your life. Now we would greatly encourage you to study the Word of God on a weekly, and even daily, basis. To continue your study of the Bible we invite you to consider other books in the Knowing the Bible series and to visit www.knowingthebible series.org.

Lastly, take a moment again to look back through this study. Review again the notes that you have written, and the things that you have highlighted or underlined. Reflect again on the key themes that the Lord has been teaching you about himself and about his Word. May these things become a treasure for you throughout your life—this we pray in the name of the Father, and the Son, and the Holy Spirit. Amen.

Definitions

[1] **Lord** – Someone superior in authority or status to another, similar to "master." This term is a common translation for several different Hebrew titles for God in the OT, and in the NT it is often used for Jesus. When spelled in the OT with small capital letters (LORD) it translates the Hebrew "Yahweh" (YHWH), "I AM," the personal name of God.

[2] **Judgment** – An assessment of something or someone, especially moral assessment. The Bible also speaks of a final day of judgment when Christ returns, when all those who have refused to repent will be judged (Rev. 20:12–15).

KNOWING THE BIBLE STUDY GUIDE SERIES

Experience the *Grace* of God in the *Word* of God, Book by Book

Series Volumes

- Genesis
- Exodus
- Leviticus
- Numbers
- Deuteronomy
- Joshua
- Judges
- Ruth and Esther
- 1-2 Samuel
- 1-2 Kings
- 1-2 Chronicles
- Ezra and Nehemiah
- Job
- Psalms
- Proverbs
- Ecclesiastes
- Song of Solomon

- Isaiah
- Jeremiah
- Lamentations, Habakkuk, and Zephaniah
- Ezekiel
- Daniel
- Hosea
- Joel, Amos, and Obadiah
- Jonah, Micah, and Nahum
- Haggai, Zechariah, and Malachi
- Matthew
- Mark
- Luke

- John
- Acts
- Romans
- 1 Corinthians
- 2 Corinthians
- Galatians
- Ephesians
- Philippians
- Colossians and Philemon
- 1-2 Thessalonians
- 1-2 Timothy and Titus
- Hebrews
- James
- 1-2 Peter and Jude
- 1-3 John
- Revelation

crossway.org/knowingthebible